Quick & Easy

THE BOOK OF
MISO SOUP

JOIE, INC

OVERSEAS DISTRIBUTORS

UNITED STATES: JP TRADING, INC.
    400 Forbes Blvd., Unit 3
    South San Francisco, CA 94080
    Phone: (650) 871-3940
    Fax: (650) 871-3944
U.S.A.: A.K. HARANO COMPANY
U.S.A.: MASA T. & ASSOCIATES
U.S.A.(HAWAII): HAKUBUNDO, INC.
GUAM, SAIPAN AND MICRONESIAN ISLANDS: FUJIWARA'S SALES AND SERVICE
CANADA: MILESTONE PUBLICATIONS
MEXICO: EDITORIAL SAYROLS, S.A. DE C.V.
COLOMBIA: JORGE E. MORALES & CIA. LTDA.
SINGAPORE: MPH DISTRIBUTORS (S) PTE. LTD.
MALAYSIA: MPH DISTRIBUTORS SDN, BHD.
PHILIPPINES: NATIONAL BOOK STORE, INC.
INDONESIA:TOKO BUKU HARAPAN
INDIA:DANI BOOK LAND, Mumbai(Bombay)14
AUSTRALIA: BOOKWISE INTERNATIONAL
THAILAND: CENTRAL BOOKS DISTRIBUTION, LTD.
KOREA: TONGJIN CHULPAN MUYEOK CO., LTD.
TAIWAN:FORMOSAN MAGAZINE PRESS, INC.
HONG KONG: APOLLO BOOK COMPANY, LTD.

ISBN4-915831-93-0

CONTENTS

INTRODUCTION

Of all the popular cuisines of Japan, *miso*-based soup may be the easiest and the most versatile dish to cook at home. *Miso* soup used be — and still is — essential not only for the Japanese table, but for people's health.

A tablespoon of *miso*, which is the amount usually added to a cup of soup, provides about one-sixth of the protein needed per day. It is also rich in vitamins and minerals, low in fat and is easily digested as any fermented food is. The common truth is that any *miso* is rich in high quality protein which can be utilized easily in the body. This is because all kinds of protein are broken down into digestible amino acids in the process of fermentation. Besides, soy beans contain linoleic acid which acts to reduce cholesterol. Other components include vitamin E which slows aging, saponin and iso–flavone which keep the body from oxidizing. *Miso* has numerous varieties and it is hard to tell the flavor by its appearance just like cheese is in the West. However, almost any kind of *miso* can be used for soups.

The Japanese-style meal planning places emphasis on vegetables as you can find in this book, which has contributed to the amazing longevity of the people. With *miso* soup, you can consume a great variety of vegetables at one time. Once you get the knack of it, you can even make different version every day. Each recipe is planned for two servings so that you can easily multiply according to the number of persons served. Cutting technigues at the end of the book also can help you shorten the cooking time.

We sincerely recommend that you enjoy these savory, nutritious, and warming soups regularly for breakfast, lunch or any meal.

DIETETICS ON *MISO* SOUP

The humid and warm climate of Japan has created unique original foods and seasonings through fermentation just as Westerners have cheese, wine, or yogurt. Soy sauce, *miso*, and *natto* are made from fermented soybeans, and among them *miso* is called an art of microorganism because of its complicated, delicate balance of ingredients and processing. Since olden times there is a saying ,"*Miso no hattoku*", meaning *miso* has eight virtues. This explains to us that people have noticed the benefit of *miso* from experience long before modern dietetics was discussed. This old belief has been proven scientifically, as which is shown in the following chapter.

The Japanese used to keep a simple diet of "one soup and one dish" to accompany a bowl of rice. "One dish" changed from simmered vegetables to grilled fish, depending on the region, economic or seasonal conditions whereas *miso* soup was never left out whatever the conditions. Such a simple combination of food has created small but tough, healthy bodies of the Japanese. Now the world is focusing on our diet, especially on *miso* soup, the mainstay.

Nutritional Value of *Miso*

To describe the benefit of *miso* soup, we will study a little about *miso*. Various types of *miso* are on the market today. Although each product differs in the local conditions, ingredients and fermentation period, the basic ingredients are common: soybeans (1), *koji* starter(2), and salt (3).

(1) Soybeans are rich in high quality proteins outshining other vegetables. This is why we call them "meat from the field". In fact, soybeans provide a much wider variety of nutrients in comparison with meat. Carbohydrates in soybeans contain more dietary fiber than meat. Soybeans are rich in unsaturated fatty acids while meat contains lots of saturated fatty acids. They have no cholesterol, but have trace elements such as vitamins and minerals that do not exist in meat.

(2) *Koji* starter is added in a small amount, but it is a very hardworking mold. This starter, Aspergillus, attaches to boiled or steamed grains such as rice, barley, or soybeans, and produces enzymes of many kinds. These enzymes work to break down proteins into peptides, and some of them are further broken down into more digestible amino acids. Carbohydrates are partially broken down into D-glucose, and fat is broken down into fatty acids and glycerine. These substances created by fermentation add to the nutritious character to *miso*.

(3) The amount of salt in *miso* is around 10 %, depending on the product. This ratio is necessary to inhibit the increase of harmful bacteria while activating lactic acid bacteria and yeast. Once *miso* soup was regarded as an "enemy" of health because of its high salt content. *Miso* soup should be regarded not as a salty water but as a nutrient source in addition to the ingredients added to the soup.

The main ingredients above work each other to create nutrients that are essential to the body.

Figure 1. **Comparative Table of Nutrients in 3½oz(100 g) beef and soybeans(dried)**

Content / Food			Beef	Soybean
Energy value (kcal)			238	417
Protein (g)			18.5	25.3
Fat (g)			16.9	19.0
Fatty acids	total (g)		14.9	16.67
	saturated (g)		6.62	2.57
	unsaturated	mono-unsaturated (g)	7.89	3.61
		poly-unsaturated (g)	0.44	10.49
Cholesterol (mg)			65	ϕ
Carbohydrates	sugar (g)		0.2	23.7
	fiber (g)		0	17.1
Ash (g)			0.9	5.0
Minerals	sodium (mg)		55	1
	potassium (mg)		290	1900
	calcium (mg)		5	240
	magnesium (mg)		0	220
	phosphorus (mg)		150	580
	iron (mg)		2.3	9.4
	zinc (mg)		0	3.20
	copper (μg)		0	980
Vitamins	oil-soluble	A effect (Iμ)	43	ϕ
		E (mg)	0.3	1.8
		K (μg)	ϕ	18
	water-soluble	B$_1$ (mg)	0.08	0.83
		B$_2$ (mg)	0.20	0.30
		B$_6$ (mg)	0.21	0.53
		B$_{12}$ (mg)	28	0
		niacin (mg)	3.6	2.2
		C (mg)	2	ϕ

Source: Standard Tables of Food Composition in Japan,
    4th Revised Edition
Note: Dried soybeans will weigh 2.5 times when reconstituted.

Benefits of *Miso* as a Fermented Food

The process of fermentation creates some substances that the original ingredients, soybeans and grains, do not contain. These elements function as anti-cancer and anti-aging agents, and reduce cholesterols as well. For example, digestible amino acids and vitamin E contained in *miso* help to make the walls of blood vessels smooth and soft and as a result encourage the circulation of blood in the body and brain cells. Lecithin works to prevent forgetfulness in the aged, caused by poor blood circulation. Vitamin B group works to prevent high blood pressure and abnormal contraction of the blood vessels, caused by nicotine. In such cases, it is likely to be more effective if eaten with *wakame* or *natto* as an ingredient of *miso* soup.

Another benefit as a fermented food is that the bacteria in *miso* has broken down proteins before your own enzyme system does in the body. Proteins need time to be digested in the body, but *miso* has turned into digestible amino acids. These amino acid contain active digestive enzyme which helps digest other food taken in at the same time.

Miso as a Food for Function

Recently Japanese government has announced that some foods have a third function besides the common uses as nutrient source to support life, and as a pleasure source. This extra function includes protection of the body from diseases, to recover from diseases, or to prevent aging.

Miso is a good example of a food with the third function, and it has been proven first in 1945 when the atomic bomb fell on Nagasaki. Dr. Akizuki, the director of St. Francisco Hospital, worked hard for years to save lives of those who were affected by radiation. He wondered why he and his hardworking staff had not shown any expected effects of radiation. He later reported that it was probably because his staff had *miso* soup daily. At that time his hospital was also used as the City's warehouse for *miso* and soy sauce to supply the citizens, and therefore the staff could regularly eat *miso* soup with *wakame* seaweed.

Later, Dr. Akira Ito of Atomic Radiation Institute of Hiroshima Univ., certified, after experiments on animals, that *miso* acts to eliminate radioactive materials. It is well known that after the accidents at Chernobyl and Three Mile island, there was a rush of orders for *miso* from all over the world. In 1981 his report was further proven by Dr. Hirayama of National Cancer Center when he announced that those who take *miso* soup daily have much less possibility of getting stomach cancer than those do not. The research was carried out on 2,600,000 subjects for 13 years.

Well, this excellent food does have good effects on the human body, but do not think its benefits are instantaneous. Try to include *miso* in your daily menu and take it in regularly for your health.

Figure 2: **Table of Effective Composition of *Miso***

Soybean	**Protein**	Lowering cholesterol, Maintaining elasticity of the arteries , Preventing stroke
	Vitamin E	Reducing LDL cholesterol formation, Preventing aging
	Saponin	Reducing LDL cholesterol formation, Reducing blood cholesterol, Preventing hardening of the arteries, Preventing liver diseases
	Trypsin inhibitor	Anti-cancer action, Preventing diabetes
	Iso-flavone	Anti-oxidation, Soothing stiff shoulders, Preventing breast cancer
	Lecithin	Lowering cholesterol, Preventing hardening of the arteries, Preventing senile dementia
	Choline	Preventing fatty liver
	Brown pigment	Preventing LDL cholesterol formation, Preventing aging
	Dietary fiber	Cholesterol lowering, Preventing intestinal cancer
Koji starter	**Vitamin B$_2$**	Promoting deoxidation of the body
Bacteria	**Vitamin B$_{12}$**	Producing blood, Preventing nerve strain
Koji, enzyme, lactic acid bacteria	**Oxygen**	Helping digestion
Linoleic acid from soybean	**Prostaglandin E**	Preventing high blood pressure

HOW TO MAKE *MISO* AT HOME

INGREDIENTS
1 lb(450 g) dried soybeans
9½ oz(270 g) rice *koji*
6 oz(170 g) natural sea salt
About ⅓ cup soybean-boiling water

1 Place soybeans in a large bowl, cover with ample water and let stand overnight.

2 Transfer soybeans with soaking water into a pot. Bring to a boil, then reduce heat and simmer about 2 hours, frequently skimming.

3 When beans are tender, transfer into a grinding bowl. Crush beans with a pestle using a pounding motion. Save the water used for boiling.

4 When the beans begin to stick to the mortar, stir in reserved water and salt. Stir until evenly mixed.

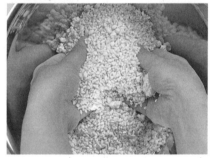

5 In a bowl, crumble rice *koji* using your fingers.

6 Add finely crumbled *koji* to the mortar, a small amount at a time. Mix with a spatula using a cutting motion.

7 When mixed evenly, put the paste into a sealable plastic bag. Press out as much air as possible.

8 Place the bag in an airtight container and cover tightly. It is recommended you mark the container with the date. Store in a cooler corner of the kitchen or in a cellar, out of direct sunlight.

9 Once or twice a month, uncover and press out air. If *tamari* (thick soy sauce) forms on the surface, stir in evenly. Let ferment for about 6 months or more.

MISO MAP OF JAPAN

Miso was introduced into Japan from China over 1300 years ago, and since then it has developed in so many ways to suit the local conditions that today you can't find "chiang," the original variety of Chinese *miso*, anywhere in this country. Instead, there are uncountable varieties of *miso* in every district of Japan.

Although *miso* is a simple mixture of soybeans, *koji*, salt and water, it can be classified in into many ways — by ingredient, by taste, by color, by birthplace, or by texture. If categorizing according to ingredients, there are *kome*(rice) *miso*, *mame* (soybean) *miso*, and *mugi* (barley) *miso*.

Name of *miso* stands for the type of *koji* starter

The character of *miso* depends on *koji* starter, a fermenting agent. 80% of commercial *miso* uses rice grains to make the *koji* and is called *kome*(rice) *miso*. It has a wide range of varieties depending on the ratio of *koji* and salt, from light to dark colored, and sweet to salty.

As you go north, the saltiness and the darkness of *miso* seems to increase gradually. If you divide the country in half, people of Kansai, or western area, love light-colored, sweeter *miso*, whereas darker and salty type is preferred by the residents of warmer, eastern area. Sweet *mugi* (barley) *miso* is mainly favored in the very south, especially in Kyushu island.

Mugi miso, or barley *miso*, is made from barley *koji*, and it originated in farmers' households where *miso* was made with their crop of barley or oat. Therefore it has another name, *inaka*(country) *miso*, and this variety is still popular in many districts.

Mame miso, or soybean *miso*, has handed down the origin of *miso* itself, and is made with the help of its own *koji*. Soybeans are boiled, crushed, and formed into blocks, then hung outdoors until a mold forms on the surface.

The farmers washed and soaked the dried blocks in water overnight, then pounded them with salt and water before storing in wooden tubs to let them mature. *Mame miso* is dark red in color, and has distinctive, rich flavors with a subtle bitterness. Today, this method is only found in remote areas, but several varieties are made commercially and sold under the names of *Hatcho*, Nagoya, *sanshu* or *akadashi miso*.

The color of *miso* does not always indicate its flavor

Although it is quite difficult to classify *miso* by the color, we usually divide them into two colors — *shiro*(light-colored) *miso* and *aka*(dark-colored) *miso*. Light-colored *miso* includes creamy white *saikyo miso,* the darkest one includes *akadashi miso*. The brown color of *miso* is created by a chemical reaction in the process of maturation. The protein of soybeans and its natural amino acids react with the sugar content, and the color darkens in time. It darkens as the storing temperature rises and as the maturing period is longer. Dark-colored *miso* is made of steamed soybeans and needs time to mature while light-colored type needs approximately two weeks until it matures, and its sugar content is released in the process of boiling, preventing the darkening as a result.

Blending of *miso*

Miso gourmets often use their own blends of two or more *misos* for the soup. When two types made of different *koji* are mixed, the taste is mellowed, and a new flavor is obtained.

Regional dishes using *miso*

■**CHAN CHAN YAKI from Hokkaido**
Settlers in Hokkaido, the northern island, used to wash their spades and cooked the day's catch on them.These meals usually consisted of salmon or cod, along with vegetables and seasoned *miso*.

■*HOTO* **from Yamanashi**
A general name for soup with flour noodles or dumplings. Pumpkin is a must among various vegetable ingredients. Handmade "pasta" is stewed in lightly flavored *miso* soup.

■*MISO NIKOMI UDON* **from Aichi**
Udon, or thick noodles, are cooked in *miso* soup without parboiling, together with chicken, long onion, and fried *tofu*. Haccho *miso* is used especially in this area.

■*DOTE NABE* **from Hiroshima**
Oyster soup cooked on the table. Hiroshima is known for good quality oysters, and they are seasoned with *miso*, which is formed into an embankment(*dote*) around the edges of an earthenware pot and gradually dropped into the broth.

■*YAKI MISO* **from Tokushima**
Savory relish made of *miso*, sugar and *yuzu* citron juice boiled down into a smooth paste. It is often served in *yuzu* cups.

■*HOBA YAKI* **from Gifu**
Miso and herbs are grilled over charcoal, using a thick leaf of Japanese magnolia as a pan and it is favored as an excellent appetizer. A miniature stove is used on the table to enjoy the mixed bouquets.

TENJIN-SAN **from Kyoto** (See page 68)
SATSUMA-JIRU **from Kagoshima** (See page 69)
GOKO-JIRU **from Mie** (See page 70)
DONGAME-JIRU **from Kyoto** (See page 70)
NATTO-JIRU **from Yamagata** (See page 71)
TORORO-JIRU **from Saitama** (See page 71)
TSUMIRE-JIRU **from Chiba** (See page 72)
TON-JIRU **from Kanto Area** (See page 73)
UCHIKOMI-JIRU **from Kagawa** (See page 73)
KASU-JIRU **from Iwate** (See page 74)
DONGARA-JIRU **from Yamagata** (See page 74)
ISHIKARI NABE **from Hokkaido** (See page 75)
ITOKO-JIRU **from Kyoto** (See page 76)
DANGO-JIRU **from Oita** (See page 77)

Hokkaido *miso* (Hokkaido)
Salty, reddish brown *miso*. Hokkaido *miso* has a standard flavor so as to adjust the immigrants from all over Japan.

Tsugaru *miso* (Aomiri)
Salty, brown *miso*. Rich in flavor from long maturation.

Akita *miso* (Akita)
Salty dark brown *miso*. It has higher content of *koji* than common *kome miso*.

Hiroshima *miso* (Hiroshima)
Sweet, light yellow *miso* with rich and deep flavor resembling *saikyo miso* of Kyoto.

Echigo *miso* **& Sado** *miso* (Niigata)
Salty dark-colored *miso*. Echigo type has grains of rice. Sado type has a rich aroma.

Sendai *miso* (Miyagi)
Typical type of salty and dark-colored *miso*. Because of long-term maturation, the salt is mellowed and the flavor is deep.

Setouchi *mugi miso* (Ehime, Yamaguchi, Hiroshima)
Barley *miso* with a sweet flavor, made in the area close to Kyushu, the main producing area.

Kaga *miso* (Ishikawa)
Salty dark-colored *miso* made with long term maturaiton. Developed as a military provisions of Maeda Clan of Kaga.

Aizu *miso* (Fukushima)
Salty dark-colored *miso*. Aromatic flavor from long-term maturation.

Hokkaido

Yamagata

Tokyo

Yamanashi

Kyoto

Hiroshima

Tokushima

Fukuoka

Kagoshima

Sanuki *miso* (Kagawa)
Very sweet, light yellow *miso* with deep and rich flavor.

Kyushu *mugi miso* (Kyushu area)
Sweet, light-colored barley *miso*. Each prefecture has products with its own character.

Gozen *miso* (Tokushima)
Sweet, dark-colored *miso* with higher ratio of *koji*. This type *miso* enhances any ingredients.

Kansai *shiro-miso* (Kinki area)
Very sweet, light yellow *miso* used widely in cooking. The sweetest variety is known as *saikyo miso*.

Tokai *mame miso* (Aichi, Gifu, Mie)
Soybean *miso* with unique, rich aroma with a subtle bitterness. Known under names such as *Hatcho*, Nagoya, or *sanshu miso*.

Shinshu *miso* (Nagano)
Salty light-colored *miso*. Shinshu type makes up 40 % of total production of the country.

Edo *ama-miso* (Tokyo)
Sweet, dark red *miso* with a distinctive fragrance. This is the only sweet type *miso* in Kanto area.

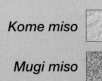

Kome miso

Mugi miso

Mame miso

9

MISO SOUP
COOKING
BASICS

Until just recently, there was a saying that when a young woman has learned
how to make delicious *miso* soup, she is qualified to become a bride.
Today it is obsolete of course, partly because *miso* soups have become very easy
to cook thanks to the instant *dashi* stock and/or *miso* that contains *dashi*.
Miso soup is still a staple for everyday meals enjoyed regardless of the meal styles and
the time of the day. When the Japanese think of the word *miso*, however,
the first image that comes to mind would be piping hot *miso* soup in a lacquerware bowl.
Although *miso* soup is a simple mixture of *miso* and *dashi* stock,
you can widen your choice by altering the key ingredients.
In order to make delicious *miso* soup, it is useful to know about them.

MISO — VARIETIES & USAGE

Usually light-colored *miso* is less salty than the dark-colored type, but there are always exceptions. Here are several samples to show you the typical character of each variety. Try several types and find your favorite combination.

**Light-colored *miso*
(smooth)**

Can be called white(*shiro*) *miso* in comparison with red (*aka*) *miso*. The actual color is creamy beige as shown here. Usually mellow in flavor, it enhances delicate ingredients such as white fish, *tofu*, and some vegetables.

**Light-colored *miso*
(with grains)**

Dark-colored *miso* (smooth)

Darker in color, this type *miso* has a rich flavor and generally tastes saltier than light-colored type. Great for meats or fish.

Blended *miso* (with grains)

When making *miso* soup, we often blend two or more varieties of *miso* to improve the flavor. There is no strict rules of which to blend with which, but usually we add 2 part dark *miso* with 1 part light-colored type. Generally it is good to blend ones from distant areas.

Akadashi miso

Reddish brown to chocolate colored *miso*, made mainly of steamed and crushed soy beans. The aromatic, rich, and slightly bitter flavor of this gourmet *miso* adds its special fragrance to soups and other dishes. *Hatcho miso* is one of the name brands of this type.

Mugi miso

This type of *miso* originated in southern areas because local farmers used the barley from their abundant crops to make homemade *miso* with its subtle sweetness, *mugi miso* still has individual differences depending on the district.

Saikyo miso

Typical yellow(white) *miso* originated in Kyoto. Boiled soy beans are mixed with double amount of rice *koji* starter to create a rich sweetness and creamy texture. Popular on winter tables for its sweetness and richness.

DASHI STOCK — INGREDIENTS & METHODS

Dashi stock is another essential element for tasty *miso* soup. Each method here requires no special technique or experience. All you have to do is time it right. Read the directions before you actually cook to assure success. Feel free to combine any kinds of *dashi*, since there are no strict rules which *dashi* to use for which ingredient.

【*KATSUO DASHI*】

Dried bonito flakes gives a plain, delicate flavor which brings out subtle flavor of vegetables and *tofu*. Flakes of mackerel or tuna are also used in the same manner.

Serves 2
3 sachets (½ oz/15 g)
   katsuobushi flakes
2 cups water

1 Bring the water to a rapid boil, and add the flakes at once.

2 Immediately turn off heat. Let stand until the flakes settle at the bottom of pan.

3 Line a colander with paper towels that have been wet and wrung out, and strain. Do not press or squeeze fish flakes.

【*KOMBU DASHI*】

Kombu kelp creates a mild and plain *dashi* which enhances seafood ingredients in soup whereas other *dashi* makes the soup "heavy" to your palate.

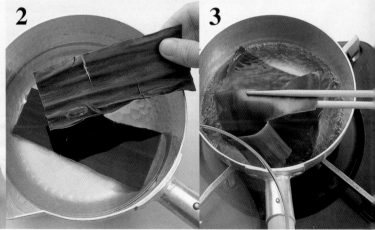

Serves 2
2 2" x 4"(5 cm x10 cm)
   cuts *kombu*
2 cups water

1 Using a length of paper towel that has been wetted and well wrung out, wipe the surfaces of *kombu*. Using scissors, make several slits into sides.

2 Place *kombu* and water in a saucepan and let stand until *kombu* becomes tender and larger, for about 30 minutes.

3 Place over low heat. When the water starts to bubble, take out *kombu* before a complete boil is reached.

【IRIKO DASHI】

Dried sardines (*niboshi*) provide a deep savory flavor and gives richness to *miso* soup. Cleaning of the fish can be done well ahead of time. Heads and guts are removed before use.

Serves 2
7-8 dried sardines
2 cups water

1 Snip off head and intestines of fish. Split lengthwise and rinse briefly with water.

2 Place sardines and water in a saucepan. Let stand at least 1 hour. Cook over medium heat and bring to a boil. Cook 10 minutes, occasionally skimming off floating scum.

3 Line a colander with a wetted and tightly wrung paper towel and strain stock.

【INSTANT DASHI】

Today all kinds of *dashi* are available in powder, granules, or "tea bag" style. Although they might not quite the same as the ones made from scratch, as you can imagine, they are too convenient to refuse if making for *miso* soups.

Powder or granule type
Instant *dashi* often comes in tiny pouches. By adding to boiling water, you can prepare savory stocks. Be careful so as not to add too much since most products have stronger and saltier flavor than natural *dashi*. Here's a secret to upgrade the flavor: Add a few drops of *sake*.

Tea bag type
These are more "natural" than granules yet less bothersome than traditional methods. Ingredients are crushed and sometimes blended with different ones such as *shiitake* to give the best flavor. Add to boiling water and cook for 3-5 minutes before taking out or follow the directions on the package.

【ICHIBAN DASHI】

This is called the primary stock because it is reputed to have the finest flavor. After making *kombu dashi*, add dried bonito flakes to the boiling stock and turn off heat. It goes with any ingredients, often used for delicate clear soups.

STORING DASHI

Although it is ideal to make *dashi* every time, you can make a large batch and freeze it in airtight containers or freezer bags. The flavor keeps for 10 to 14 days. Leftover stock may be stored in the same way.

HOW TO MAKE MOST OF YOUR *MISO*

The final trick to making *miso* good-tasting soup is not difficult, but is simply to get the timing right. Here are some useful hints to draw out the best flavor from your *miso*.

Dissolving *miso*

Although you can blend *miso* paste and some stock in a ladle using a fork or whisk, there is a more surefire way to make the soup even and smooth. *Misokoshi*, or *miso* strainer, comes with a small head and a handle so that you can dip the paste into hot stock to stir and dissolve it easily.

Place measured *miso* in the strainer and dip into the stock. Stir gently with a ladle or attached pestle.

Add or discard grains according to your liking.

Never boil *miso* soup

Reduce heat when adding *miso*, and turn off heat when it shows signs of boiling. The fragrant aroma will be lost if it is boiled vigorously.

Also, when reheating leftover *miso* soup, turn off or remove from heat just before it reaches the boiling point. If a member of your family wants to eat later, save stock so that *miso* can be added just before serving.

Storing *miso*

Despite its humble appearance, *miso* is very delicate and easily deteriorates or discolors if stored improperly. Once you have opened the package, be sure to shut out the air and store well sealed container in the refrigerator. It is ideal to purchase a small portion at a time especially when dealing with the sweet *saikyo miso*. Unopened *miso* keeps for months at room temperature.

Miso in plastic container

 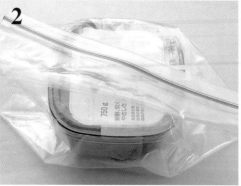

Cover the surface of *miso* with attached paper, and replace lid.

Put the container in a sealed plastic bag and refrigerate.

Miso in plastic bag

Let air out and close the opening tightly. Put in an airtight container and refrigerate.

MISO SOUP GARNISHES

A pinch of garnish can upgrade the impression of the simple *miso* soup. Here are some spices and herbs that are added commonly in Japan. Make a good choice by considering both the flavor and the season. Spicy garnishes would warm you up in cold weather, and rich soups with meat or fish can be lightened with ginger or onion. *Kinome* heralds spring with its strong fragrance. Other seasonal garnishes include *yuzu* citron rind or *myoga* buds.

Sesame seeds

Either black or white seeds gives richness to soups. For even richer flavor, use ground seeds.

Sansho pepper

Also called Japanese pepper, this powder releases a zesty fragrance and is effective when you want a change from your everyday soup.

Black pepper

Use freshly ground peppercorn, or choose a coarsely ground product.

Seven spice mix

A blend of seven spices: *shichimi togarashi* contains red pepper, *sansho* pepper, sesame seeds, dried mandarin peel, hemp seeds, poppy seeds and *aonori*(green laver).

Scallion

Enjoy the refreshing fragrance and the vivid color. Sliced and frozen scallions make an emergency garnish.

Long onion

Long onion, or Tokyo *negi*, is often sliced and soaked in water to remove the biting flavor. Spring onion can be used as well.

Shiso leaves

Popular tender leaves called beefsteak plant. The attractive, tangy flavor improves your appetite. There is no substitute.

Fresh ginger

Great for both cold and hot weather as it goes very well with *miso* soups by adding a refreshing taste. Powdered ginger does not compare.

Kinome

Young *sansho* sprigs. The distinctive, minty taste can be further enhanced by slapping between your palms.

Hot mustard

Karashi, or Japanese hot mustard paste, contains no vinegar, and comes in a tube which increases the life up to a year. Great in cold weather.

15

VEGETABLE COMBOS

A bowl of *miso* soup can greatly increase daily intake of vegetables
which we tend to neglect due to the bother of preparations.
Most of the ingredients here are cooked in a single saucepan,
and the vegetables decrease in volume when they are cooked,
enabling you to take much more nutrients and dietary fiber than you would expect.

POTATO
CARROT
BROCCOLI
CABBAGE

Serves 2
1 small potato
⅓ carrot
¼ head broccoli
1 large cabbage leaf
1½ cups *dashi* stock
1½-2 Tbsp light-colored *miso*

92 kcal per serving

1 Cut potato and carrot into ¼"(6 mm) thick
quarter rounds. Soak potato in water.
2 Divide broccoli into florets. Slice cabbage leaf:
core into thin slices, leaf into shreds.
3 In a saucepan, place stock, carrot, and drained
potato, and bring to a boil.Reduce heat to medium
and when almost cooked, add broccoli and
cabbage. Cook for a further 2-3 minutes.
4 Soften *miso* in a ladle, by adding 1 Tbsp stock
from the pan and blend using a wire whisk or fork.
Stir into stock. Remove from heat as soon as it
reaches the boiling point. Serve immediately.

ASPARAGUS CARROT
Shiitake mushroom
Tofu

Serves 2
6 spears asparagus
2 *shiitake* mushrooms
⅓ carrot
⅓ cup crumbled *tofu*
1 fried *tofu(abura-age)*
1½ cups *dashi* stock
1½-2 Tbsp light-colored *miso*

105 kcal per serving

1 Remove hard ends of asparagus. Peel about ¾"(2 cm) from the ends and cut into 1" (2.5 cm)lengths.
2 Cut off stems from *shiitake*, and slice thinly. Peel and slice carrot thinly, lengthwise.
3 To remove excess oil from fried *tofu*, place it in a bowl and pour boiling water over it. Then slice thinly.
4 In a saucepan, cook stock and carrot. Bring to a boil and reduce heat to medium. When carrot is tender, add all ingredients except *tofu*, and cook 1-2 minutes.
5 Soften *miso* in a ladle, by adding 1 Tbsp stock from the pan and blending with a wire whisk or fork. Gradually add softened *miso* to the stock. Add crumbled *tofu*. Remove from heat as soon as it reaches the boiling point.

Vegetable preparation

In this chapter various kinds of vegetables are introduced as *miso* soup ingredients to provide good vitamins and minerals.

To prepare greens, be sure to remove yellowish leaves and wash carefully until they are free from sand or soil. If thick or tough, make a crisscross slit into the root end. Bring ample water to a rapid boil and add root ends first for most greens. When cooking *komatsuna* and garlic chive, put leaf ends in first since their other ends are more tender. Adjust cooking time to your liking. It is advisable to parboil only briefly for *miso* soups.

Plunge into cold water and squeeze out water well. Cut according to need. It is a good idea to wrap the cooked and cut greens in plastic film and freeze until needed.

SPINACH
SATOIMO POTATO
Yuba

Popular Ingredients

Yuba

Yuba, a delicacy in Japanese cuisine, is another soybean product. It is a thin film of soy fat, skimmed from boiling soy milk in the process *of tofu* making. It can be served as a special *sashimi*, but is usually dried for long storage. *Yuba* is treasured for its delicate flavor and texture.

Serves 2

½ pack spinach
3 *satoimo* potatoes
1 sheet dried *yuba* (see right)
1½ cups *dashi* stock
1½-2 Tbsp dark-colored *miso*

90 kcal per serving

1 Parboil spinach briefly and plunge into water before the color fades. Cut into 1"-1½"(2.5 cm-4 cm) lengths.
2 Peel *satoimo* potatoes and slice into ¼"(6 mm) thicknesses. Rub with 1 Tbsp salt to remove sliminess, and rinse in water.
3 Soak dried *yuba* in water, and tear into bite-size pieces.
4 In a saucepan place stock and *satoimo* potatoes. Bring to a boil and reduce heat to medium. Cook until *satoimo* slices are tender.
5 Add spinach and *yuba*, and cook for 1 minute.
6 Dissolve *miso* as for previous page, and remove from heat as soon as it reaches the boiling point.

Peeling *satoimo* **potatoes**
Uncooked *satoimo* potatoes may prove irritating to the skin. This can be prevented by drying *satoimo* potatoes before peeling.

Serves 2

½ long onion(Tokyo *negi*)
½ bunch *wakegi*
½ pack
  nameko
  mushrooms
⅓ cake soft
  tofu
1 egg, beaten
1½ cups *dashi* stock
1½-2 Tbsp dark-colored *miso*

120 kcal per serving

1 Slice long onion diagonally. Cut *wakegi* into 1½"(4 cm) lengths and divide into white and green parts.
2 Place *nameko* mushrooms in a small colander, and shake briefly under running water to remove excess sliminess.
3 Cut *tofu* into ⅜"(1 cm) cubes and drain.
4 Heat *dashi* stock to a boil. Add long onion, white parts of *wakegi*, and *nameko*. Cook for 2 minutes.
5 Reduce heat to medium and dissolve *miso* in stock as for page 17. Add green parts of *wakegi* and *tofu*. Return to boil.
6 Swirl in beaten egg and remove from heat when softly set.

LONG ONION
Nameko mushroom
Tofu

CHRYSANTHEMUM LEAVES
Enoki mushroom
Natto

Serves 2

1 pack chrysanthemum leaves
1 pack *enoki* mushrooms
1 small packs *natto*, optional
1½ cups *dashi* stock
1½-2 Tbsp dark-colored *miso*

144 kcal per serving

1 Cut chrysanthemum leaves into 2"(5 cm) lengths.
2 Discard rood ends of *enoki* mushrooms, and cut into half lengths. Separate if necessary.
3 Bring stock to a boil and add greens and *enoki* mushrooms.
4 Return to boil. dissolve *miso* (see page 17, #5) and add *natto*. Remove from heat as soon as it reaches the boiling point. Serve immediately.

KOMATSUNA GREENS
Tofu dumpling
Yam cake

Serves 2

½ bunch *komatsuna* greens
4 small *tofu* dumplings (*ganmodoki*)
½ yam cake (*konnyaku*)
1½ cups *dashi* stock
1½-2 Tbsp light-colored *miso*

159 kcal per serving

1 Trim away root ends of greens and cut into 1½" (4 cm) lengths.
2 Place *ganmodoki* balls in a colander, and pour over boiling water to remove excess oil.
3 Using a spoon, scrape off bite-size pieces from yam cake. Parboil briefly and drain.
4 In a saucepan, place *dashi* stock, *ganmodoki*, and yam cake Bring to a rapid boil, reduce to medium heat and cook for 3-4 minutes. Add greens and return to a boil.
5 Soften *miso* in a ladle, by adding 1 Tbsp stock from the pan and blend with a wire whisk or fork. Stir into stock. Remove from heat as soon as it reaches the boiling point. Serve immediately.

Popular Ingredients

Biography of *komatsuna* greens

Although this popular vegetable is available in any district of Japan, it originated in Komatsu River region of Edo, or old Tokyo. *Komatsuna* greens contains lots of vitamins, calcium and iron, and has no bitterness. It needs no parboiling, and its plain taste complements any other ingredients.

PEPPER
DRIED *DAIKON*

Serves 2
1 large bell pepper
¼ cup dried *daikon* radish
1 loaf *fu* (wheat gluten), optional
1½ cups *dashi* stock
1½-2 Tbsp *akadashi miso*

74 kcal per serving

1 Cut pepper into irregular, bit-size pieces.
2 Soften dried *daikon* as directed below, and squeeze lightly. Cut up.
3 Soak *fu* in water and squeeze out water.
4 In a saucepan, place stock, *daikon* and *fu*, and bring to a boil. Lower heat to medium and cook for 1-2 minutes. Add pepper and return to boil.
5 Dissolve *miso* in the stock (see page 17, #5).

(**Popular Ingredients**)

Kiriboshi daikon (dried *daikon* radish)

Shredded and dried *daikon* is sold in bags as *kiriboshi daikon*. It keeps long and is convenient for soups, salads, and other simmered dishes. To prepare, soak in water to just cover, for 10-20 minutes. Use lukewarm water when in a hurry.

GOYA GOURD
BEAN SPROUT
Tofu

Serves 2
¼ large *goya*
½ package bean sprouts
½ cake *tofu*
1½ cups *dashi* stock
1½-2 Tbsp light-colored *miso*

83 kcal per serving

1 Split *goya* lengthwise, and scoop out seeds and membrane with a spoon. Cut into 1/8"(3 mm) slices.
2 Remove roots from bean sprouts.
3 Bring *dashi* stock to a boil, and cook *goya* and bean sprouts for 1-2 minutes.
4 Soften *miso* in a ladle by blending with 1 Tbsp stock from the pan. Gradually dissolve in stock. Tear *tofu* into bite size and add to the pan. Turn off heat as soon as it reaches the boiling point.

(**Popular Ingredients**)

Goya gourd

This prickled looking gourd is a popular ingredient in Okinawa and China. Its bitterness is favored for its nutritious value. To reduce bitterness, remove the inside completely and rub with salt.

STRING BEAN PUMPKIN EGGPLANT

Serves 2

2 oz(60 g) green beans
3 oz(100 g) pumpkin
1 Japanese eggplant or ¼ regular eggplant
½ fried *tofu (abura-age)*
1½ cups *dashi*
1½-2 Tbsp *akadashi miso*

94 kcal per serving

1 Remove strings from green beans and cut into 1"(2.5 cm) lengths. Cut pumpkin into ¼"(6 mm) slices or bite-size pieces. Slice eggplant and soak in water.
2 In a small bowl, place fried *tofu* and pour over boiling water to remove excess oil; cut into small triangles.
3 In a saucepan, place stock, pumpkin, and eggplant, and bring to a boil. Reduce heat to medium and add green beans and fried *tofu*. Cook just until the pumpkin is tender.
4 Soften *miso* in a ladle, by adding 1 Tbsp stock from the pan and blend using a wire whisk or fork. Stir into stock. Remove from heat as soon as it reaches the boiling point. Serve immediately.

ONION
ASHITABA GREENS
Dried shrimp

Serves 2
1 bunch *ashitaba* greens
½ onion
¼ cup dried shrimp
1½ cups *dashi* stock
1½-2 Tbsp dark-colored *miso*

64 kcal per serving

1 Trim off tough ends of greens, and cut up.
2 Cut onion into ⅜"(1 cm) thick wedges.
3 In a saucepan, place stock and onion, and bring to a boil. Reduce heat and cook until onion is transparent. Add greens and cook briefly.
4 Soften *miso* in a ladle, by adding 1 Tbsp stock from the pan and blend using a wire whisk or fork. Stir into stock. Remove from heat as soon as it reaches the boiling point. Serve immediately.

Popular Ingredients

Ashitaba greens

Ashitaba literally means tomorrow greens, because it bears a new leaf the day after it being picked. It is known for its high content of vitamins and minerals.

Nutritional value of *miso* soup and how to reduce salt content

Nutritional value of *miso* depends on its main ingredient — rice, barley, or soybeans.

The common truth is that any *miso* is rich in high quality protein which can be utilized easily in the body. It is because all kinds of protein are broken down into digestible amino acids in the process of fermentation.Besides, soybeans contain linoleic acid which acts to reduce cholesterol. Other contents include vitamin E which prevents aging, saponin and iso-flavone which keep the body from oxidizing.

The only worry when taking *miso* daily would be the salt content. Salt is necessary in producing *miso* and the final product has 5% to 12 % salt. However, the amount used for soup is diluted by the addition of water and other ingredients, so the final concentration is only 1 %. The best way to reduce salt intake is to decrease *miso* ratio by increasing the amount of ingredients such as seaweeds or vegetables, so as to decrease the salty liquid.

It may not known well that *miso* is expected to help prevent not only from stomach cancer but also from illnesses caused by atomic radiation. See page 6 for details.

SEAFOOD WITH VEGETABLES

Seafood adds a savory flavor when used in *miso* soups.
Seafood *miso* soup can be a substitute for a main dish by adjusting the amount.

CLAMS
Asparagus
Potato

Serves 2
½ lb(230 g) short neck clams in shell
3 spears asparagus
1 small potato
1 ½ cups *dashi* stock
1 ½-2 Tbsp light-colored *miso*

94 kcal per serving

1 Remove sand from clams (see below). Clean the shells and drain.
2 Trim off tough ends of asparagus, and peel around ends. Slice diagonally.
3 Cut potato into bite-size pieces, and soak in water.
4 In a saucepan place stock, clams and drained potato, and bring to a boil. Remove scum and cook until the shells open.
5 Add asparagus and cook briefly. Dissolve *miso* in small amount of stock from the pan, then stir in. Turn off heat as soon as it reaches the boiling point.

Preparations of short neck clams
In-shell short neck clams need to be soaked in water as salty as sea water to let out sand. Dissolve 1 Tbsp salt in 2⅓ cups of water and immerse clams for 2-3 hours or overnight in a dark place. Wash well before using.

CRAB
Trefoil
Gobo burdock
Enoki mushroom

Serves 2

2 small crabs
½ bunch trefoil (*mitsuba*)
⅓ *gobo* burdock
½ package *enoki* mushrooms
1 long onion (Tokyo *negi*)
1½ cups *kombu* stock
3 Tbsp *sake*
2 Tbsp light-colored *miso*

139 kcal per serving

1 Cut up crabs. Cut trefoil into 1"-1½"(2.5 cm-4 cm) lengths.
2 Scrape off skin of *gobo* and slice diagonally; soak in water for 15 minutes changing water once.
3 Trim off root ends of mushrooms. Cut as for trefoil. Cut long onion into same lengths.
4 In a saucepan bring stock and *sake* to a boil. Add crab, *gobo*, mushrooms and long onion. Cook for 7-8 minutes, occasionally skimming scum that floats.
5 When crab is cooked, dissolve *miso* gradually. Simmer and return to a gentle boil. Turn off heat and top with trefoil.

How to choose and prepare fish

When buying fish fillets, check that there is no liquid that the fish has released from being thawed in the package. Also check if the flesh is shiny and resilient. Seafood makes the broth flavorful if used as a *miso* soup ingredient. It is advisable to do a little preparation before adding fish to the pot. Place fish fillets cut into bite-size pieces in a colander, and douse with boiling water until the surface turns whitish, then plunge into cold water and drain well. This process removes the odor of the fish making the soup delicious.

Seafood such as squid, octopus, prawn, and other shellfish needs no such preparation.

SQUID
Wakame seaweed
Ginger

Serves 2

1 small squid
$\frac{1}{12}$ oz(2 g) dried *wakame* bits
1 long onion (Tokyo *negi*)
1 knob ginger
1$\frac{1}{2}$ cups *dashi* stock
1$\frac{1}{2}$-2 Tbsp light-colored *miso*

77 kcal per serving

1 Pull out legs of squid and cut off the inside. Clean body cavity and remove transparent cartilage. Slice into rings. Cut remainings into bite-size pieces.
2 Soak *wakame* in water to soften and squeeze out water.
3 Slice long onion diagonally. Shred ginger.
4 Bring stock to a boil and add all vegetables. Return to boil and dissolve *miso*. Turn off heat as soon as it reaches the boiling point.

CORBICULAE
Lettuce
Long onion

Serves 2

$\frac{1}{2}$ lb(230 g) corbiculae
$\frac{1}{4}$ head lettuce
$\frac{1}{2}$ long onion (Tokyo *negi*)
1$\frac{1}{2}$ cups *kombu* stock
1$\frac{1}{2}$ Tbsp *akadashi miso*

64 kcal per serving

1 Clean corbiculae(see page 24) and drain.
2 Tear lettuce leaves into bite-size pieces.
3 Slice long onion.
4 In a saucepan heat stock and corbiculae to a boil.Cook until the shells open,skimming away any scum.
5 Add lettuce and long onion, and return to boil. Dissolve *miso*, and turn off heat at the boiling point.

PRAWN
Onion
Snow pea

Serves 2
6 prawns, shelled
1 oz(30 g) snow peas, strung
1½ cups *dashi* stock
1½-2 Tbsp light-colored *miso*

75 kcal per serving

1 Devein prawns and cut a deep slit along each back.
2 Slice onion thinly.
3 Cut large snow peas in half, if any.
4 In a saucepan heat stock and onion to a boil. Reduce heat to medium and cook for 2-3 minutes.
5 Add prawns and cook. Add snow peas and return to boil.
6 Dissolve *miso* and turn off heat when reaching the boiling point.

SALMON
Cauliflower
Bean vermicelli

Serves 2
1 fillet salmon
½ head cauliflower
⅓ oz(10g) bean vermicelli
1½ cups *kombu* stock
1 tsp *sake*
1½-2 Tbsp light-colored *miso*

140 kcal per serving

1 Cut salmon into bite-size pieces. Prepare ice water in a bowl. Place salmon pieces in a colander and pour over boiling water, then plunge into ice water and drain. (See page 25)
2 Soak bean vermicelli in lukewarm water until supple; cut into bite-size lengths. Divide cauliflower into florets.
3 In a saucepan heat stock, *sake*, salmon, and cauliflower to a boil. Reduce heat to medium and cook for 4-5 minutes.
4 Add bean vermicelli and return to boil. Dissolve *miso* and turn off heat as soon as it reaches the boiling point.

OCTOPUS
Tomato
Parsley
Garlic

Serves 2

3 oz(100 g) boiled octopus
2 tomatoes
1 sprig parsley
1 clove garlic
1 long onion
1 tsp olive oil
1½ cups *dashi* stock
1½-2 Tbsp dark-colored *miso*

108 kcal per serving

1 Slice octopus thinly.

2 Peel tomato: Broil over flame or blanch in boiling water; plunge into ice water and peel. Cut into half horizontally and remove seeds. Cut into bite-size pieces.

3 Slice garlic thinly. Cut long onion into quarters lengthwise, then into ¾" (2 cm) lengths.

4 Heat olive oil in a saucepan, and fry garlic until aroma is released. Stir in tomato and long onion.

5 Add stock and bring to a boil. Add octopus and parsley. Dissolve *miso* and turn off heat as soon as it reaches the boiling point.

SQUID
Eggplant
Shiitake mushroom

Serves 2
1 small squid
1 Japanese eggplant
4 *shiitake* mushrooms
1½ cups *dashi* stock
1½-2 Tbsp dark-colored *miso*

74 kcal per serving

1 Pull out legs of squid and cut off the inside. Clean body cavity and remove transparent cartilage. Peel skin and cut open. Make shallow scores in lattice pattern, and cut into 1"(2.5 cm) squares. Peel and cut remainings into bite-size pieces.
2 Cut eggplant into 6 wedges, then into 1"(2.5cm) lengths. Soak in water for 5 minutes.
3 Slice mushrooms.
4 In a saucepan place stock and drained eggplant, and bring to a boil. Cook briefly and add squid. Finally add mushrooms.
5 Dissolve *miso*. Turn off heat when reaching the boiling point.

MACKEREL
Daikon radish
Spinach
Ginger

Serves 2
1 small fillet mackerel
3 oz(100 g) *daikon* radish
2-3 bunches spinach
1 knob ginger
1⅔ cup *kombu* stock
2 Tbsp dark-colored *miso*

161 kcal per serving

1 Cut mackerel into 1"(2.5 cm) thick pieces. Place in a a colander and pour over boiling water and plunge into ice water (see left).
2 Cut spinach into bite size lengths. Cook briefly in boiling water; plunge into cold water and squeeze out moisture.
3 Cut *daikon* lengthwise into quarters, then into thin slices. Shred ginger.
4 In a saucepan, place stock, mackerel, *daikon* and ginger, and bring to a boil. Reduce heat and cook for 5-6 minutes.
5 Add spinach and return to the boil. Soften *miso* in a ladle blending with 1 Tbsp of stock from the pan. Gradually dissolve in remaining stock. Turn off heat as soon as it reaches the boiling point.

PRAWN
Shimeji mushroom
Freeze-dried *tofu*
Yam cake

Serves 2

4 prawns
1 package *shimeji* mushrooms
½ oz(15 g) snow peas
⅓ yam cake (*konnyaku*)
½ freeze-dried *tofu* (*koya-dofu*)
1⅔ cups *dashi* stock
1 Tbsp light-colored *miso*
1 Tbsp dark-colored *miso*

92 kcal per serving

1 Shell and devein prawns. Trim off root ends of mushrooms and divide into clusters.
2 String snow peas and cut diagonally into 3 to 4.
3 Cut yam cake into ⅜"(1 cm) cubes and parboil. Soften freeze-dried *tofu* in water, squeeze out and cut into same size cubes.
4 In a saucepan place stock, yam cake and freeze-dried *tofu*. Bring to a boil and cook prawns. Lastly add snow peas.
5 Immediately dissolve *miso* in stock and turn off heat as soon as it reaches the boiling point.

(**Popular Ingredients**)

Freeze-dried *tofu*

This preserved *tofu* is called *koya-dofu* since it was widely used in the famous *zen* temple of Mt. Koya. Also called *kori-dofu* or *shimi-dofu*,both meaning "frozen"*tofu*. This type *tofu* has a different texture and flavor than regular *tofu*, and has been favored as a good source of protein. Add to seasoued stock directly and simmer until softened for about 15 minutes.

Serves 2
3 oz(100 g) boiled octopus
3 oz(100 g) sweet potato
1 stalk thick celery
1½ cups *dashi* stock
1½-2 Tbsp light-colored *miso*

132 kcal per serving

1 Cut octopus diagonally into ⅛"(3 mm) slices.
2 Cut sweet potato unpeeled into rolling wedges (see page 89); soak in water.
3 String celery and cut as for sweet potato.
4 In a saucepan place stock and drained sweet potato. Bring to a boil, then reduce heat to medium. Cook just until the potato is tender.
5 Add celery and cook briefly. Add octopus and dissolve *miso* into stock. Turn off heat as soon as it reaches the boiling point.

OCTOPUS
Celery
Sweet potato

COD
Tofu
Chinese cabbage

Serves 2
1 fillet fresh cod
½ cake *tofu*
3 oz(100 g) Chinese cabbage
1 oz(30 g) scallions
1⅔ cups *kombu* stock
2 Tbsp *sake*
2 Tbsp light-colored *miso*

139 kcal per serving

1 Cut cod into bite-size pieces. Blanch in boiling water, then plunge into cold water and drain.
2 Slice *tofu*. Slice Chinese cabbage diagonally so the cut edges absorb the flavor well. Cut scallions into 2"(5 cm) lengths.
3 In a saucepan place stock, *sake*, cod and Chinese cabbage, and bring to a boil. Reduce heat to medium and cook for 5-6 minutes.
4 Dissolve *miso* gradually into stock. Add scallions and *tofu*. Turn off heat when reaching the boiling point.

MEAT & POULTRY WITH VEGETABLES

Pork, beef or chicken makes a quite filling soup,
and adds more savory flavor to the *dashi* stock.
Make a good combination with vegetables of your choice.

PORK
Boston lettuce
Egg

Serves 2
3 oz(100 g) thinly sliced pork
½ Boston lettuce
½ medium carrot
2 eggs
1½ cups *dashi* stock
1½-2 Tbsp dark-colored *miso*

172 kcal per serving

1 Tear lettuce into 2 or 4 pieces, the core attached.
2 Slice carrot into ⅛"(3 mm) slices. Cut pork into bite-size pieces.
3 In a saucepan place stock and carrot. Bring to a boil and add pork slices. Removing scum, cook until heated through. Break egg into a small bowl and gently drop into the stock so as not to damage the yolk. Cook for 4-5 minutes or until desired doneness is achieved.
4 Add lettuce, then dissolve *miso*. Turn off heat when reaching the boiling point.

CHICKEN DUMPLING
Shimeji mushroom
Japanese turnip
Carrot

Serves 2

Chicken dumplings
- 3 oz(100 g) ground chicken
- 2 tsp *sake*
- 1 knob ginger, minced
- 2"(5 cm) length long onion
  (Tokyo *negi*), minced
- 2 Japanese turnips(*kabu*)
- ⅓ medium carrot
- ½ package *shimeji* mushrooms
- 1⅔ cups *dashi* stock
- 2 Tbsp light-colored *miso*

199 kcal per serving

1 In a bowl, mix chicken dumpling ingredients.
2 Cut off greens from turnips, leaving ½"(1.5cm) stems attached to turnips. Cut into wedges and wash carefully to remove dirt between stems. Cut greens into 1"(2.5cm) lengths. Trim off root ends of *shimeji* mushrooms and divide into clusters.
3 Cut carrot lengthwise into thin rectangles.
4 In a saucepan place stock, turnips and carrot, and bring to a boil. Drop some chicken mixture forming into a ball with hands or a spoon. Return to boil, reduce to medium heat, and cook for 7-8 minutes. Add turnip greens.
5 Dissolve *miso* and turn off heat when reaching the boiling point.

Meat for *miso* soup

A small amount of meat or poultry gives *miso* soup a rich flavor. When adding meat to the pot, be sure to remove the floating scum as it will spoil the flavor.

As for serving, *miso* soups with meat should be warmed up so as to tenderize the tissues of the meat.

Consider the procedure of cooking

Miso soup is usually cooked in a single pot. Since cooking time differs depending on each ingredient and its cutting method, be sure to cut tough vegetables such as carrot, into thin slices or shreds, and add them to the pot in the first place.

Fast cooking ingredients such as *tofu* and *wakame* can wait until *miso* is dissolved in the stock.

PORK
Gobo burdock
Long onion

Serves 2
3 oz(100 g) thinly sliced pork
½ *gobo* burdock
1 long onion(Tokyo *negi*)
1 tsp sesame oil
1½ cups *dashi* stock
1½-2 Tbsp dark-colored *miso*

163 kcal per serving

1 Scrape off *gobo* and rinse under tap water. Cut into shavings. Soak in water to remove harshness, changing water.
2 Slice long onion diagonally.
3 In a saucepan heat sesame oil. Stir-fry drained *gobo* until supple. Add pork slices and stir-fry. Add stock and bring to a boil.
4 Reduce heat to medium and cook for a further 1-2 minutes, occasionally removing scum. Dissolve *miso*, and turn off heat when reaching the boiling point.

GROUND CHICKEN
Pumpkin
Shimeji mushroom

Serves 2
3 oz(100 g) ground chicken
3 oz(100 g) pumpkin
1 package *shimeji* mushrooms
1 Tbsp *sake*
1½ cups *dashi* stock
1½-2 Tbsp dark-colored *miso*

182 kcal per serving

1 Discard seeds of pumpkin, and peel partially. Slice into ¼"(6 mm) thick, bite-size pieces.
2 Trim off root ends of *shimeji*.
3 In a saucepan place stock and pumpkin, and bring to a boil. Reduce heat and cook until pumpkin is tender.
4 Combine ground chicken with *sake*. Add to the pot, and skim away the scum when boiled. Add *shimeji* and cook briefly.
5 Dissolve *miso*. Turn off heat when reaching the boiling point.

BEEF
Bok choy
Maitake mushroom

Serves 2
3 oz(100 g) thinly sliced beef
2 small bok choys
1 package *maitake* mushroom
1½ cups *dashi* stock
1½-2 Tbsp light-colored *miso*

129 kcal per serving

1 Cut bok choy in half. Cut stalk part into 8 wedges. Cut up leaves.
2 Tear *maitake* into clusters.
3 Bring *dashi* stock to a boil. Add beef slices and return to the boil. Remove scum and add bok choy and *maitake*. Cook briefly.
4 Dissolve *miso* and turn off heat when reaching the boiling point.

GROUND PORK
Molokheiya
Nameko mushroom

Serves 2
3 oz(100 g) ground pork
1 package molokheiya
1 package *nameko* mushrooms
1½ cups *dashi* stock
1½-2 Tbsp dark-colored *miso*

180 kcal per serving

1 Cut molokheiya into bite-size pieces. Wash *nameko* lightly and drain.
2 Bring *dashi* stock to a boil. Add ground pork and crumble. Reduce heat to medium and remove scum. Add molokheiya and cook briefly.
3 Dissolve *miso* and turn off heat when reaching the boiling point.

(**Popular Ingredients**)

Molokheiya
Widely used in Mid-East, this nutritious vegetable contains lots of vitamins and iron. When cooked, it emits a slippery substance. Do not overcook if adding to *miso* soup.

CHICKEN WINGTIP
Kombu
Daikon radish
Carrot

Serves 2
4 chicken wingtips
2 oz(60 g) shredded fresh *kombu*
3 oz(100 g) *daikon* radish
½ long onion(Tokyo *negi*), sliced
⅓ carrot
1⅔ cups *kombu* stock
2 Tbsp *sake*
2 Tbsp light-colored *miso*

200 kcal per serving

1 Onto back side of chicken wingtip, make a deep incision along bone.
2 Cut *daikon* and carrot into ⅜" × 1½"(1 cm × 4 cm) sticks.
3 In a saucepan place stock, chicken, *kombu* and *daikon*. Bring to a boil and remove scum. Reduce heat to medium and cook for 15 minutes.
4 When chicken is tender, dissolve *miso* gradually. Add sliced long onion. Turn off heat when reaching the boiling point.

GROUND PORK
Cucumber
Eggplant

Serves 2
3 oz(100 g) ground pork
1 Japanese cucumber
1 eggplant
½ cake thick fried *tofu* (*atsu-age*)
1½ cups *dashi* stock
1½-2 Tbsp *akadashi miso*

252 kcal per serving

1 Cut cucumber and eggplant into rolling wedges. Soak eggplant in water to remove harshness.
2 Place thick fried *tofu* in a colander, pour over boiling water to remove excess oil. Cut into bite-size pieces.
3 In a saucepan place *dashi* stock, drained eggplant, fried *tofu*, and bring to a boil. Add ground pork, and break up into pieces. Remove scum. Add cucumber, and cook briefly.
4 Dissolve *miso* gradually. Turn off heat as soon as it reaches the boiling point.

BEEF
Peppers
Garlic chives

Serves 2
3 oz(100 g) thinly sliced beef
1 each red and yellow pepper
½ bunch garlic chives
½ long onion (Tokyo *negi*)
1½ cups *dashi* stock
1 Tbsp dark-colored *miso*
½ Tbsp light-colored *miso*

130 kcal per serving

1 Cut pepper into rolling wedges. Cut garlic chives and long onion diagonally into ⅜"(1 cm) slices.
2 Heat stock to a boil, and add beef slices. Remove scum. Add all vegetables and cook for 3-4 minutes.
3 Dissolve *miso* in stock, and turn off heat as soon as it reaches the boiling point.

CHICKEN
Daikon radish
Daikon greens

Serves 2
½ chicken thigh (about ¼ lb/120 g)
5 oz(150 g) *daikon* radish with leaves
1¾ cups *dashi* stock
2 Tbsp light-colored *miso*

150 kcal per serving

1 Cut chicken into bite-size pieces.
2 Cut *daikon* radish into rolling wedges.
3 Discard outside leaves of *daikon* and use central tender part. Cook in boiling water, and plunge into cold water; squeeze and cut up.
4 In a saucepan place stock and *daikon*, and bring to a boil. Add chicken and return to boil. Remove scum and reduce heat. Cook for 10 minutes until tender, then dissolve *miso* in stock.
5 Add *daikon* greens, and turn off heat as soon as it reaches the boiling point.

Popular Ingredients

Azuki beans
Small red beans now available in cans. Just drain and add to soups. Do not use *yude-azuki*, a sweetened type.

BEEF
Lotus root
Azuki beans

Serves 2
3 oz(100 g) thinly sliced beef
2 oz(60 g) lotus root
⅓ cup canned *azuki* beans
1 long onion(Tokyo *negi*)
1 knob ginger
1½ cups *dashi* stock
1½-2 Tbsp light-colored *miso*

212 kcal per serving

1 Cut lotus root into rolling wedges, and soak in water for 5 minutes.
2 Cut long onion into ¾"(2 cm) lengths. Shred ginger.
3 In a saucepan place *dashi* stock and beans, and bring to a boil. Add beef and heat through. Remove scum. Add drained lotus root, long onion and ginger, and cook for 3-4 minutes.
4 Dissolve *miso* in stock, and turn off heat as soon as it reaches the boiling point.

Serves 2
½ chicken breast (about ¼ lb/120 g)
⅙ oz(5 g) *hijiki* seaweed
⅓ cup canned soybeans
½ carrot
2 tsp sesame oil
1½ cups *dashi* stock
1½-2 Tbsp dark-colored *miso*

262 kcal per serving

1 Rinse *hijiki* and soak in water for at least 30 minutes.
2 Crush soybeans into coarse bits using a morter or fork. Shred carrot. Cut chicken into bite-size pieces.
3 Heat sesame oil in a saucepan, stir-fry *hijiki*. Stir in soybeans. Add stock and bring to a boil. Reduce heat and remove scum. Cook for 2-3 minutes.
4 Dissolve *miso* in stock and turn off heat as soon as it reaches the boiling point.

CHICKEN
Hijiki seaweed
Soybeans

CHICKEN FILLET
Mushrooms
Long onion

Serves 2
2 chicken fillets
2 *shiitake* mushrooms
1 package *maitake* mushrooms
1 package *shimeji* mushrooms
½ long onion (Tokyo *negi*)
1½ cups *dashi* stock
1½-2 Tbsp *akadashi miso*

84 kcal per serving

1 Trim off cartilage from chicken fillets,and slice diagonally.
2 Trim off root ends of *maitake* and *shimeji*. Separate into clusters. Trim off stems of *shiitake* and cut into 1"(2.5 cm) slices.
3 Slice long onion thinly.
4 Heat *dashi* stock to a boil, and add mushrooms. Return to boil and add chicken to heat through.
5 Dissolve *miso* in stock, and add sliced long onion. Turn off heat as soon as it reaches the boiling point.

PORK
Sweet potato
Chinese cabbage

Serves 2
3 oz(100 g) thinly sliced pork
3 oz(100 g) sweet potato
3 oz(100 g) Chinese cabbage
1¾ cups *dashi* stock
2 Tbsp dark-colored *miso*

172 kcal per serving

1 Slice sweet potato into ¼"(6 mm) rounds or half moons. Soak in water to remove harshness for about 10 minutes.
2 Cut Chinese cabbage into thin rectangles.
3 In a saucepan place *dashi* stock and sweet potato, and bring to a boil. Add pork slices and heat through. Remove scum. Reduce heat to medium and cook for 4-5 minutes. Add Chinese cabbage and cook briefly.
4 Dissolve *miso* in stock and turn off heat as soon as it reaches the boiling point.

(**Popular Ingredients**)
Nutritious value of pork
People in Okinawa are known for longevity and it is said that one of the reasons is that they are fond of pork dishes. Pork is rich in vitamin B1 which helps food turn into energy. Lack of this vitamin often causes tiredness. Eat more pork and stay healthy.

CHICKEN LIVER
Mushrooms
Scallion

Serves 2
5 oz(150 g) chicken livers
1 package *maitake* mushrooms
1 package *enoki* mushrooms
¼ cup sliced scallions
1½ cups *dashi* stock
2 Tbsp *sake*
1½-2 Tbsp light-colored *miso*

145 kcal per serving

1 Cut up and clean chicken livers.
2 Trim off root ends of mushrooms, and separate into clusters.
3 Heat *dashi* stock and *sake* to a boil, and add livers. Return to boil and remove scum. Reduce to medium heat and cook for 7-8 minutes.
4 Add mushrooms and heat through. Dissolve *miso*, then add scallions. Turn off heat when reaching the boiling point.

BEEF
Yamato-imo yam
Spinach

Serves 2
3 oz(100 g) thinly sliced beef
3 oz(100 g) *yamato-imo* yam
2 oz(60 g) spinach
2 *myoga* buds, optional
1½ cups *dashi* stock
1½-2 Tbsp dark-colored *miso*

157 kcal per serving

1 Peel *yamato-imo* and soak in lightly vinegared water for about 10 minutes. Rinse off slippery substance and dry with a paper toweling. Put in a plastic bag and pound lightly into large chunks.
2 Cook spinach briefly and cut into 1½"(4 cm) lengths. Split *myoga* buds.
3 Heat *dashi* stock to a boil, and cook beef slices. Remove scum. Add vegetables and return to boil.
4 Dissolve *miso* in stock and turn off heat as soon as it reaches the boiling point.

SEA VEGETABLES

Sea vegetables such as *wakame* or *nori* contain almost no calories,
yet are quite filling and nutritious.
Meat or poultry can be added in combination with other vegetables
if you are weight conscious.

WAKAME
Shimeji mushroom
Maitake mushroom
Bamboo shoot

Serves 2
⅙ oz(5 g) dried *wakame* bits
½ package *shimeji* mushrooms
½ package *maitake* mushrooms
2 oz(60 g) canned bamboo shoot
¾ oz(50 g) snow peas
1½ cups *dashi* stock
1½-2 Tbsp dark-colored *miso*

38 kcal per serving

1 Trim off root ends of mushrooms, and separate into clusters. Slice bamboo shoot very thinly and parboil.
2 String snow peas.
3 Heat *dashi* stock to a boil, and add mushrooms. When heated through, add dried *wakame* and snow peas. When *wakame* bits are reconstituted, dissolve *miso* and turn off heat.

Popular Ingredients

Maitake mushroom
It literally reads "dancing" mushroom in Japanese, but don't think the mushroom dances! This aromatic mushroom used to be so rare that people who found one after a long walk in the mountains could not help dancing for joy, hence the name. Lately cultivated *maitake* are readily available in the market so we can enjoy its savory flavor and pleasant texture. Tastes good in fried or simmered dishes.

TORORO KOMBU
Daikon radish
Bamboo shoot
Scallion

Serves 2

1/10 oz (3 g) *tororo kombu* kelp
3/4 oz (50 g) *daikon* radish
1/2 carrot
1 oz(30 g) bamboo shoot
1/4 cup sliced scallions
1 1/2 cups *dashi* stock
1 1/2-2 Tbsp light-colored *miso*

43 kcal per serving

1 Cut *daikon* and carrot into julienne strips. Slice bamboo shoot into very thin slices and parboil.
2 Slice scallions.
3 In a saucepan place *dashi* stock, *daikon* and carrot, and bring to a boil. Reduce heat to medium and cook for 3-4 minutes.
4 Dissolve *miso*, and add scallions just before removing from the heat.
5 Place in serving bowls, and top with *tororo kombu*.

⬭ Popular Ingredients

Varieties of sea vegetable

Kaiso, or sea vegetable includes *nori*, *kombu* kelp, *wakame*, *hijiki*, *mozuku*, and *tosaka-nori*. They are rich in minerals such as iodine, calcium and iron. Among various kinds of sea vegetables, *wakame*, *kombu* and *hijiki* are sold in various forms. Here are some varieties that may help you choose the right product.

Salted *wakame*

Fresh *wakame* is boiled and then preserved in heavy salt. This type should be refrigerated. To use, rinse off salt and soak in water for about 5 minutes or until expanded to 6-7 times of original volume.

Dried *wakame*

Sundried or air-dried *wakame*. This type *wakame* keeps indefinitely, but needs more time to soften than salted type. Sold whole or cut-up and packed in small packets, ready to use.

Mekabu

Thick and short leaves grown at the foot of large *wakame* stem. Fresh *mekabu* is sold in early summer. Usually eaten as a salad: Shred and plunge in boiling water, then drain. Serve with soy sauce and dried bonito flakes.

Hayani kombu

Also dried but thinner *kombu* kelp is used mainly in simmered dishes. Today this type *kombu* which is often sold in a knotted form for easy preparation.

Fresh *kombu*

Fresh *kombu* takes no time to prepare, and is used in various dishes. Shredded *kombu* is available today and is used in salads.

Dashi kombu

Dried thick *kombu* kelp makes an excellent *dashi* stock. This type *kombu* is called *dashi kombu* and good quality product has a fine white powder over dark colored surface, which it also provides a good aroma.

Naga hijiki

Stem part of *hijiki*. Longer and thicker than common type. Dried product should be washed and soaked in water for 10-20 minutes before cooking.

Hijiki or *Mehijiki*

Common, short and spiky *hijiki*. If using fresh type, wash under running water to remove sand and dirt before boiling in ample water.

MIXED SEA VEGETABLES
Shortneck clam

1 Bring *dashi* stock to a boil, and add dried sea vegetables.
2 When sea vegetables are soft, add drained clams and return to boil.
3 Dissolve *miso* in stock and turn off heat as soon as it reaches the boiling point.

Serves 2
⅓ oz (10 g) *kaiso* mix
2 oz (60 g) canned clams
1½ cups *dashi* stock
1½-2 Tbsp light-colored *miso*

59 kcal per serving

MIXED SEA VEGETABLES
Ground pork

Serves 2
⅓ oz (10 g) *kaiso* mix
1 oz (30 g) ground lean pork
1½ cups *dashi* stock
1½-2 Tbsp dark-colored *miso*

97 kcal per serving

1 Heat *dashi* stock to a boil and add ground pork. Quickly break pork into pieces, and remove scum.
2 Add *kaiso* mix and cook for 2-3 minutes or until softened.
3 Dissolve *miso* in stock and turn off heat as soon as it reaches the boiling point. Serve with hot mustard paste, if you prefer.

(**Popular Ingredients**)

Kaiso mix
This is a commercially mixed dried sea vegetables including *wakame*, *sugi-nori*, *tosaka-nori*. The name of the package may say "*kaiso* salad." This kind of product can be directly added to soups without softening.

KOMBU *Daikon* radish Pork

Serves 2
6 knotted *kombu* (*musubi kombu*)
3 oz(100 g) *daikon* radish
2 oz(60 g) thinly sliced pork
1½ cups *dashi* stock
1½-2 Tbsp dark-colored *miso*

83 kcal per serving

1 Soak knotted *kombu* in water for 10-20 minutes.
2 Cut daikon into ⅛"(3 mm) thick quarter rounds.
3 Cut pork into bite-size pieces.
4 In a saucepan place *dashi* stock, *kombu* and *daikon*, and bring to a boil. Add pork slices and heat through. Remove scum and reduce heat to medium.

5 Simmer for 7-8 minutes until *kombu* becomes tender. Dissolve *miso* in stock and turn off heat as soon as it reaches the boiling point.

WAKAME Beef Onion

Serves 2
⅙ oz (5 g) dried *wakame* bits
2 oz (60 g) thinly sliced beef
½ medium onion
1½ cups *dashi* stock
1½-2 Tbsp light-colored *miso*

85 kcal per serving

1 Cut onion into wedges, ¼"(6 mm) at the widest part.
2 Heat *dashi* stock to a boil and add beef slices. Heat through and remove scum. Add onion and return to boil. Add dried *wakame* bits and reduce heat.
3 When *wakame* expands 6-7 times in volume and soft, dissolve *miso* in stock and turn off heat as soon as it reaches the boiling point.

MEKABU WAKAME
Satoimo potato
Chicken

Serves 2
3 oz(100 g) *mekabu*, shredded
1 large *satoimo* potato
2 chicken fillets (about 2 oz/60 g)
2 Chinese cabbage leaves
1½ cups *dashi* stock
1½-2 Tbsp *akadashi miso*

95 kcal per serving

1 Cut *satoimo* into quarter wedges lengthwise. Cut crosswise in half.
2 Divide Chinese cabbage; cut leaves into bite-size squares, and centers into 1"(2.5 cm) long, ⅜"(1 cm) wide strips.
3 Slice chicken diagonally into thin slices.
4 In a saucepan place stock and *satoimo*, and bring to a boil. Reduce heat and cook until *satoimo* is tender.
5 Add chicken and heat through. Add Chinese cabbage and cook briefly. Dissolve *miso* in stock and add *mekabu* just before removing from the meat.

Mekabu wakame

Helpful hint: Use a small saucepan for two

Take a small saucepan when making *miso* soup for two. A milk pan with scales on the side would be a good choice so you won't have to measure the same amount of water each time you cook.

MOZUKU
Satoimo potato
Mushrooms

Serves 2
1 packet (1¾ oz/50 g) *mozuku*
2 *satoimo* potatoes
½ package *nameko* mushrooms
½ package *enoki* mushrooms
1½ cups *dashi* stock
1½-2 Tbsp dark-colored *miso*

65 kcal per serving

1 Rinse *mozuku* in ample water and drain in a colander.
2 Rinse *nameko* and drain. Trim off root ends of *enoki* mushrooms and separate into clusters.
3 Slice *satoimo* into 1/4"(6 mm) thicknesses.
4 Place stock and *satoimo* in a saucepan and bring to a boil. Reduce heat and cook until *satoimo* is tender. Add mushrooms and return to boil. Finally add *mozuku*.
5 Dissolve *miso* in stock and turn off heat as soon as it reaches the boiling point.

FRESH *KOMBU*
Pork
Onion

Serves 2
3 oz(100 g) shredded fresh *kombu*
2 oz(60 g) thinly sliced pork
½ medium onion
1 knob ginger
1½ cups *dashi* stock
1½-2 Tbsp light-colored *miso*
1 tsp toasted sesame seeds, optional

100 kcal per serving

1 Cut up shredded *kombu* and pork slices.
2 Shred ginger. Slice onion thinly.
3 Heat *dashi* stock to a boil, add pork and return to boil. Remove scum and add ginger and onion.
4 Add *kombu* and cook briefly. Dissolve *miso* in stock and turn off heat as soon as it reaches the boiling point. Sprinkle with toasted sesame seeds, if preferred.

FRESH *KOMBU*
Carrot
Gobo burdock

Serves 2
3 oz(100 g) shredded fresh *kombu*
⅓ medium carrot
2 oz(60 g) *gobo* burdock
½ package *enoki* mushrooms
1½ cups *dashi* stock
1½-2 Tbsp light-colored *miso*

82 kcal per serving

1 Cut up shredded *kombu*. Shred carrot. Scrape off skin of *gobo*, and cut into shavings just like sharpening a pencil. Soak *gobo* shavings in water.
2 Trim off root ends of *enoki* mushrooms, and separate into clusters.
3 In a saucepan place stock, carrot and *gobo*, and bring to a boil. Reduce heat and cook for 5-6 minutes until *gobo* is tender.
4 Add *enoki* mushrooms and *kombu*, and cook for 1-2 minutes. Dissolve *miso* in stock and turn off heat as soon as it reaches the boiling point.

HIJIKI
Carrot
Fried *tofu*

Serves 2
⅓ oz(10 g) dried *hijiki*
⅓ medium carrot
½ fried *tofu* (*abura-age*)
⅓ bunch garlic chives
1½ cups *dashi* stock
1½-2 Tbsp light-colored *miso*

69 kcal per serving

1 Rinse *hijiki* in water and soak in 15-20 minutes; drain.
2 Cut carrot into thin rectangles. Remove excess oil of fried *tofu* by pouring over boiling water. Cut into rectangles. Cut garlic chives into 1"(2,5cm) lengths.
3 Bring stock and all ingredients except garlic chives to a boil, then reduce heat.
4 When carrot is tender, add garlic chives. Dissolve *miso* in stock and turn off heat just before it reaches the boiling point.

NORI
Daikon radish
Sweet potato

Serves 2
1 sheet *nori* (*yaki-nori*)
2 oz(60 g) *daikon* radish
1 oz(30 g) green beans
1½ cups *dashi* stock
1½-2 Tbsp light-colored *miso*

68 kcal per serving

1 Cut *daikon* into about ¼"(6 mm) cubes. Cut sweet potato into ¼"(6 mm) thick quarter rounds, and soak in water.
2 String green beans, and slice diagonally into 1⅛"(3 cm) lengths.
3 In a saucepan place stock, *daikon* and drained sweet potato, and bring to a boil. Reduce heat and cook until sweet potato is tender. Add green beans.
4 Dissolve *miso* in stock and add toasted *nori* torn into pieces. Turn off heat.

AONORI
Cauliflower
Turnip

Serves 2
2 oz(60 g) fresh *aonori*
3 oz(100 g) cauliflower
1 Japanese turnip (*kabu*)
1/3 cake firm *tofu*
1½ cups *dashi* stock
1½-2 Tbsp light-colored *miso*
Seven spice mix, optional

89 kcal per serving

1 Rinse *aonori* in water, and drain in colander. Separate cauliflower into florets. Trim away greens of turnip, with 1"(2.5 cm) stems attached. Cut into 6 wedges.
2 Place *dashi* stock and vegetables in a saucepan, and bring to a boil. Reduce heat and cook for 3-4 minutes.
3 Add *tofu* crushed into bite-size pieces, and return to boil. Add drained *aonori* and heat through. Dissolve *miso* in stock and turn off heat. Sprinkle with seven spice mix, if preferred.

NON-TRADITIONAL INGREDIENTS

Miso soup is a nutritiously balanced, compact food served nearly every day on Japanese tables. This chapter introduces unusual combinations of ingredients that you would not find at restaurants. Try these filling *miso* soups daily for your health.

KIMCHEE
Satoimo potato
Garlic chives

Serves 2
2 oz(60 g) kimchee (see below)
3 *satoimo* potato
2 Japanese turnips (*kabu*)
½ bunch garlic chives
1½ cups *dashi* stock
1½-2 Tbsp dark-colored *miso*

89 kcal per serving

1 Peel *satoimo* and cut into 4 wedges. Rub them with salt(extra) and rinse off slipperiness under running water. Cut garlic chives into about ¾"(2 cm) lengths. Cut kimchee into bite-size pieces.
2 Trim off stems from turnips leaving about ½"(1.5 cm) from the tops, and wash in water, removing dirt between stems.
3 Place *dashi* stock and *satoimo* in a saucepan and bring to a boil. Reduce heat to medium and cook for 3-4 minutes. Add turnips and cook until soft.
4 Add garlic chives and kimchee, then dissolve *miso* into stock. Turn off heat as soon as it reaches the boiling point.

(Popular Ingredients)

Kimchee
A general name for pickles in Korea, seasoned with chili, garlic, salt and many other ingredients. Outside Korea, the name stands for Chinese cabbage kimchee as the recipe above suggests.

COTTAGE CHEESE
Carrot
Celery

Serves 2
2 oz(60 g) cottage cheese
½ carrot
1 stalk celery
2 chicken fillets (about 2 oz/60 g)
1½ cups *dashi* stock
1½-2 Tbsp light-colored *miso*

134 kcal per serving

1 Cut carrot into thick julienne strips. String celery and cut alike.
2 Cut chicken fillets into bite-size pieces.
3 In a saucepan place *dashi* stock and vegetables, and bring to a boil. Add chicken and cook for 3-4 minutes.
4 Dissolve *miso* gradually, by thinning in a ladle with little stock from the pan. Add cheese as soon as it reaches the boiling point and turn off heat immediately.

(**Popular Ingredients**)

Cheese for *miso* soup
Cottage cheese, Parmesan cheese, or your favorite grated cheese gives a deep flavor and richness to *miso* soup. Cheese and *miso* make an unexpectedly good combination. Cook and melt cheese, or just sprinkle over soup before serving.

GRATED CHEESE
Garlic chives
Lotus root

Serves 2
1 Tbsp grated cheese
½ onion
⅓ bunch garlic chives
3 oz(100 g) lotus root
2 oz(60 g) thinly sliced pork
1½ cups *dashi* stock
1½-2 Tbsp light-colored *miso*

129 kcal per serving

1 Cut onion into wedges, ⅜" (1 cm) at the thickest width.
2 Cut garlic chives into bite-size lengths.
3 Slice lotus root into about ¼"(6 mm) widths and soak in water to remove harshness and to prevent darkening.
4 Place *dashi* stock and onion, and bring to a boil. Add pork slices and heat through, removing scum. Add vegetables and cook for 2-3 minutes until tender.
5 Dissolve *miso* in stock and turn off heat as soon as it reaches the boiling point.

(**Popular Ingredients**)

Garlic chives (*Nira*)

Also known as Chinese or coarse chives. *nira* has flat green leaves about 12"(40cm) long,and with its piquant garlic flavor, enhances meat dishes well. It is said to promote both appetite and digestion. Rich in carotene, VitaminsB1, B2, C, and other minerals that are effective for hangovers.

TUNA
Cabbage
Onion

Serves 2

3 oz(100 g) canned tuna
1 large cabbage leaf
½ onion
1 Japanese eggplant or ½ Western eggplant
1½ cups *dashi* stock
1½-2 Tbsp dark-colored *miso*

79 kcal per serving

1 Slice onion thinly. Peel eggplant lengthwise in a striped pattern, and cut into about ¼"(6 mm) slices; soak in water for 5 minutes.
2 Cut cabbage into bite-size pieces.
3 Place *dashi* stock, onion and eggplant in a saucepan, and bring to a boil. Add drained tuna and cabbage, and cook for 2-3 minutes.
4 Dissolve *miso* in stock and turn off heat just before it reaches the boiling point.

HAM
Snow pea
Potato

Serves 2

2 thick slices pork or chicken ham
2 oz(60 g) snow peas
1 small potato
1½ cups *dashi* stock
1½-2 Tbsp dark-colored *miso*

99 kcal per serving

1 Cut ham into bite-size pieces. String snow peas. Slice potato into about ¼"(6 mm) thick, quarter rounds, and soak in water.
2 Place *dashi* stock and drained potato in a saucepan, and bring to a boil. Reduce heat to medium and cook for 5-6 minutes until potato is tender. Add ham and pea pods, and cook briefly.
3 Dissolve *miso* in stock and turn off heat as soon as it reaches the boiling point.

BARBECUED PORK
Daikon radish
Long onion

Serves 2
2 slices Chinese barbecued pork
3 oz(100 g) *daikon* radish
1 long onion
1½ cups *dashi* stock
1 Tbsp dark-colored *miso*
½ Tbsp light-colored *miso*

82 kcal per serving

1 Cut long onion into 1½"(4 cm) lengths and split into quarters.
2 Slice Chinese barbecued pork into julienne strips.
3 Cut *daikon* into similar julienne strips.
4 Place *dashi* stock, pork and *daikon* in a saucepan, and bring to a boil. Add long onion and then dissolve *miso* in stock and turn off heat as soon as it reaches the boiling point.

FISHCAKE ROLL
Bean sprouts
Yam cake

Serves 2
2 small fishcake rolls (*chikuwa*)
3 oz(100 g) yam cake strips (*ito konnyaku*)
1½ cups *dashi* stock
1½-2 Tbsp dark-colored *miso*
Shiso leaves, optional

112 kcal per serving

1 Discard thread-like roots of bean sprouts.
2 Slice fishcake roll into thin rounds diagonally.
3 Cut yam cake strips into bite-size lengths, and parboil briefly.
4 In a saucepan place *dashi* stock, yam cake strips, and bring to a boil. Add bean sprouts and fishcake rolls, and cook briefly.
5 Dissolve *miso* in stock and turn off heat as soon as it reaches the boiling point. Garnish with shredded *shiso* leaves, if preferred.

【*MISO* SOUPS WITH BACON】

BACON Clam Broccoli

Serves 2
2 strips rasher bacon
½ lb (230 g) shortneck clams
¼ head broccoli
3 oz(100 g) *daikon* radish
1½ cups *dashi* stock
1½-2 Tbsp light-colored *miso*

130 kcal per serving

1 Cut bacon strips into rectangles.
2 Clean clams by rubbing each other in water; drain. (See page 24 for clam preparation)
3 Divide broccoli into small florets.
4 Cut *daikon* into thin quarter rounds.
5 Place *dashi* stock, shortneck clams and *daikon*, and bring to a boil. When clams are open, add bacon and cook for 2-3 minutes.
6 Dissolve *miso* in stock and turn off heat as soon as it reaches the boiling point.

BACON Bamboo shoot Watercress

Serves 2
2 strips rasher bacon
5 oz(150 g) boiled bamboo shoot
1 small bunch watercress
1½ cups *dashi* stock
1½-2 Tbsp dark-colored *miso*

117 kcal per serving

1 Cut bacon strips into wide rectangles.
2 Cut bamboo shoot resembling the bacon; tips into thin slices lengthwise, bottom into thin half moons crosswise. Parboil briefly.
3 Cut watercress into bite-size lengths.
4 Place stock and bamboo shoot in a saucepan, and bring to a boil. Add bacon and cook briefly.
5 Add watercress and dissolve *miso* in stock and turn off heat as soon as it reaches the boiling point.

BACON
Corn
Carrot

Serves 2
3 strips rasher bacon
1 oz(30 g) canned corn kernels
⅓ carrot
½ onion
1½ cups *dashi* stock
1½-2 Tbsp dark-colored *miso*

157 kcal per serving

1 Cut up bacon strips. Drain corn kernels. Slice carrot into thin rectangles. Slice onion thinly lengthwise.
2 Place stock and vegetables in a saucepan, and bring to a boil. Add bacon and cook for 2-3 minutes.
3 Dissolve *miso* in stock and turn off heat as soon as it reaches the boiling point.

BACON
Green bean
Cauliflower

Serves 2
2 strips rasher bacon
2 oz(60 g) green beans
¼ head cauliflower
1 sprig parsley
1½ cups *dashi* stock
1½-2 Tbsp dark-colored *miso*

107 kcal per serving

1 Cut bacon and green beans into bite-size pieces.
2 Cut onion into thin wedges. Divide cauliflower into florets.
3 Heat a saucepan and cook bacon. When fat starts to melt, add vegetables and stir-fry briefly. Pour in stock and bring to a boil. Reduce heat and cook for 2-3 minutes.
4 Add snipped parsley leaves to stock. Dissolve *miso* and turn off heat as soon as it reaches the boiling point.

BACON
Cherry tomato
Zucchini
Mushroom

Serves 2
2 strips rasher bacon
3 oz(100 g) cherry tomatoes
½ zucchini
4 button mushrooms
1½ cups *dashi* stock
1½-2 Tbsp dark-colored *miso*

109 kcal per serving

1 Cut bacon strip into ½"(1.5 cm) squares.
2 Remove tops from cherry tomatoes.
3 Cut zucchini into thin slices. Trim off root ends of mushrooms, and split into quarters.
4 Place bacon in a saucepan and heat until fat melts. Add zucchini slices and stir-fry briefly. Pour in *dashi* stock and bring to a boil. Add tomatoes.
5 Dissolve *miso* in stock and turn off heat as soon as it reaches the boiling point.

Bacon for soup

Bacon adds a richer flavor to *miso* soups as well as to Western soups or stews. If you want to strengthen the bacon flavor, cook it over low heat and fry other ingredients in its fat before adding stock. When you prefer a simple flavor, add bacon after other ingredients are cooked in stock, and simmer for a while before adding creamed *miso*.

FROZEN FOODS

There's no need to wash, peel, slice, or parboil the ingredients if you use frozen food.
Just drop them unthawed into pot, and voila!
Savory *miso* soup is ready within 10 minutes.

MEATBALL
GREEN PEA
Onion

Serves 2
6 frozen meatballs
3 oz (100 g) frozen green peas
½ onion
1½ cups *dashi* stock
1½-2 Tbsp light-colored *miso*

119 kcal per serving

1 Cut onion into wedges, about ¼"(6mm) at the widest part.
2 Heat *dashi* stock to a boil, and add unthawed meatballs and peas. Also add onion and cook for 3-4 minutes until meatballs are done.
3 Dissolve *miso* in stock and turn off heat as soon as it reaches the boiling point.

MIXED SEAFOOD
Daikon radish
Trefoil

Serves 2

5 oz(150 g) mixed seafood
    (frozen seafood)
2 oz(60 g) *daikon* radish
1 bunch trefoil (*mitsuba*)
1½ cups *dashi* stock
1½-2 Tbsp dark-colored *miso*

81 kcal per serving

1 Cut *daikon* into thin rectangles.
2 Cut *mitsuba* into about 1⅛"(3cm) lengths.
3 Place stock and *daikon* in a saucepan, and bring to a boil. When *daikon* becomes transparent, add unthawed mixed seafood, and cook for 2-3 minutes over high heat.
4 When seafood is heated through, reduce heat and dissolve *miso* in stock, making sure not to boil completely.
5 Add trefoil and turn off heat.

(**Popular Ingredients**)

Frozen seafood

Cleaned and cut seafood including clams, shrimp, and squid, ready to use in any type of dishes, stir-fried or simmered.

JAPANESE VEGETABLES
Fried *tofu*

MIXED VEGETABLES
Sausage

Serves 2

5 oz(150 g) mixed Japanese vegetables
(frozen *wafu yasai* mix)
½ fried *tofu* (*abura-age*)
1½ cups *dashi* stock
1½-2 Tbsp dark-colored *miso*

91 kcal per serving

1 Douse fried *tofu* in boiling water to remove excess oil.
2 Heat *dashi* stock to a boil and add fried *tofu* and frozen vegetables.
3 Cook over medium heat for 5-6 minutes until vegetables are tender.
4 Dissolve *miso* in stock and simmer for 1-2 minutes.

Serves 2

5 oz (150 g) mixed vegetables (frozen *on-yasai* mix)
3 wieners or 1 frankfurter
1½ cups *dashi* stock
1½-2 Tbsp dark-colored *miso*

154 kcal per serving

1 Cut wieners into bite-size pieces.
2 Heat *dashi* stock to a boil and cook frozen vegetables over medium heat for 4-5 minutes.
3 Add wieners and return to boil. Dissolve *miso* in stock and turn off heat as soon as it reaches the boiling point.

(**Popular Ingredients**)

Frozen *wafu yasai* mix

A mixture of Japanese vegetables for simmered dishes and soups, often including *shiitake* mushroom, lotus root, bamboo shoot, *satoimo* potato, carrot, green beans, etc.

(**Popular Ingredients**)

Frozen *on-yasai* mix

Assorted cut vegetables for cooking, often including cauliflower, broccoli, asparagus, carrot, etc.

CHINESE VEGETABLES
Pork

JAOZI
Garlic chives

Serves 2
5 oz(150 g) mixed Chinese vegetables
       (frozen *chuka yasai* mix)
2 oz(60 g) thinly sliced pork
1½ cups *dashi* stock
1½-2 Tbsp light-colored *miso*

78 kcal per serving

1 Cut pork into bite-size pieces.
2 Heat *dashi* stock to a boil and cook pork slices, separating pieces. Return to boil and remove scum.
3 Add frozen vegetables and cook for 3-4 minutes until heated through.
4 Dissolve *miso* in stock and turn off heat as soon as it reaches the boiling point.

Frozen *chuka yasai* mix
Assorted vegetables for Chinese stir-fried dishes, including cloud ear and *shiitake* mushrooms, bamboo shoot, carrot, snow pea, etc.

Serves 2
1 package (about 8) jaozi (pot stickers)
⅓ bunch garlic chives
1½ cups *dashi* stock
1½-2 Tbsp dark-colored *miso*
Shredded ginger, optional

112 kcal per serving

1 Cut garlic chives into about 2"(5 cm) lengths.
2 Heat *dashi* stock to a boil and cook frozen jaozi over medium heat for 4-5 minutes.
3 When jaozi are soft, add garlic chives and cook briefly. Dissolve *miso* in stock and turn off heat as soon as it reaches the boiling point. Garnish with shredded ginger, if preferred.

Frozen jaozi
Precooked Chinese dumplings known also as pot stickers. Ingredients and flavor depends on the brand.

GREEN BEAN
Satoimo potato
Carrot
Thick fried *tofu*

Serves 2

2 oz (60 g) frozen green beans
2 small *satoimo* potatoes
⅓ carrot
⅓ cake thick fried *tofu* (*atsu-age*)
1½ cups *dashi* stock
1½-2 Tbsp dark-colored *miso*

97 kcal per serving

1 Slice *satoimo* into about ¼"(6 mm) thicknesses. Cut carrot into julienne strips.
2 Douse fried *tofu* with boiling water to remove excess oil. Drain and cut into thin squares.
3 Heat *dashi* stock to a boil and cook *satoimo* until soft. Add fried *tofu* and frozen green beans (cut, if preferred); cook for 2-3 minutes until tender.
4 Dissolve *miso* in stock and turn off heat as soon as it reaches the boiling point.

No time to cook?

When you need something warm and savory at once, frozen food will be useful, especially for *miso* soup. Select parboiled and cut-up vegetables so you can just throw into the stock. It takes only a few minutes to soften.

Store other options like French fries or Chinese dim sums to enjoy a fusion of different cultures. If possible, add easy-to-cook ingredients such as scallions or *tofu* for the final touch. Tuna or ground meat also needs no preparation.

DAIKON GREENS
Freeze-dried *tofu*
Sweet potato

Serves 2
5 oz (150 g) frozen *daikon* greens
½ cake freeze-dried *tofu* (*koya-dofu*)
2 oz (60 g) sweet potato
1½ cups *dashi* stock
1½-2 Tbsp light-colored *miso*

104 kcal per serving

1 Soak freeze-dried *tofu* in lukewarm water, squeeze out water and cut into rectangles. Cut sweet potato into about ¼"(6 mm) thick, 1" (2.5 cm)long strips. Soak in water and drain.
2 Heat *dashi* stock to a boil and cook freeze-dried *tofu* and sweet potato for 4-5 minutes until sweet potato is tender. Add frozen *daikon* greens and return to boil.
3 Dissolve *miso* in stock and turn off heat as soon as it reaches the boiling point.

(**Popular Ingredients**)

Frozen *daikon* greens

Rich in vitamin A and calcium. Fresh *daikon* greens are blanched, cut up, and frozen. When using, crumble necessary portion and save the remaining. If unavailable, blanch and freeze yourself.

FRENCH FRIES
Bamboo shoot
Ham

Serves 2
3 oz(90 g) frozen French fries
2 oz(60 g) bamboo shoot (boiled)
2 slices ham
1½ cups *dashi* stock
1½-2 Tbsp light-colored *miso*
Black peppercorn

119 kcal per serving

1 Slice bamboo shoot into about ⅛"(3 mm) thicknesses, and parboil. Cut ham into bite-size pieces.
2 Heat *dashi* stock to a boil and cook unthawed French fries for 3-4 minutes.Add ham, and dissolve *miso* in stock. Turn off heat as soon as it reaches the boiling point. Sprinkle with ground black pepper, if preferred.

SPINACH CORN
Bacon

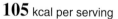

Serves 2
4 oz(120 g) frozen spinach
2 oz(60 g) frozen corn
2 strips rasher bacon
1½ cups *dashi* stock
1½-2 Tbsp light-colored *miso*

105 kcal per serving

1 Cut bacon into 1"(2.5 cm) slices.
2 In a saucepan heat *dashi* stock to a boil and cook unthawed spinach, corn and bacon for 3-4 minutes.
3 When spinach is thawed, gradually dissolve *miso* in stock and turn off heat as soon as it reaches the boiling point.

PUMPKIN
Fishcake roll
Long onion

Serves 2
5 oz(150 g) frozen pumpkin (*kabocha*)
2 small fishcake rolls (*chikuwa*)
½ long onion (Tokyo *negi*)
1½ cups *dashi* stock
1½-2 Tbsp dark-colored *miso*

122 kcal per serving

1 Slice fishcakes and long onion diagonally into same size. Cut pumpkin into bite-size pieces, if necessary.
2 Heat *dashi* stock to a boil and cook frozen pumpkin over medium heat for 4-5 minutes.
3 When pumpkin becomes tender, add fishcake and long onion, and cook briefly. Dissolve *miso* in stock and turn off heat as soon as it reaches the boiling point.

MIXED MUSHROOMS
Tuna
Parsley

Serves 2
7 oz(200 g) frozen mixed mushrooms
3 oz(90 g) canned tuna (oil-free)
2 sprigs parsley
1½ cups *dashi* stock
1½-2 Tbsp *akadashi miso*

55 kcal per serving

1 Drain canned tuna. Tear parsley leaves apart.
2 Heat *dashi* stock to a boil and cook unthawed mushrooms and tuna in it for 2-3 minutes. Add parsley and return to boil.
3 Dissolve *miso* in stock and turn off heat as soon as it reaches the boiling point.

BABY BROCCOLI
Egg
Onion

Serves 2
3 oz(100 g) frozen baby broccoli
½ onion, sliced
1 egg, beaten
1½ cups *dashi* stock
1½-2 Tbsp light-colored *miso*

112 kcal per serving

1 Heat *dashi* stock to a boil and cook unthawed greens and onion for 3-4 minutes.
2 When baby broccoli is heated through, dissolve *miso* gradually.
3 Bring to a gentle simmer, and stir in beaten egg. Turn off heat when it is barely sets.

GRILLED EGGPLANT
Ground pork
Long onion

1 Cut frozen eggplants into bite-size pieces.
2 Heat *dashi* stock to a boil and add ground pork. Separate pork and remove scum. Add eggplant and cook for 3-4 minutes.
3 When eggplants are tender, add sliced long onion. Dissolve *miso* in stock and turn off heat as soon as it reaches the boiling point.

Serves 2
2 frozen Japanese eggplants
 (grilled and peeled)
2 oz(60 g) ground pork
⅓ long onion (Tokyo *negi*), sliced
1½ cups *dashi* stock
1½-2 Tbsp *akadashi miso*

135 kcal per serving

Popular Ingredients

Frozen grilled eggplant
Small, Japanese eggplants are grilled and peeled, ready to use. If unavailable, cook fresh eggplant in a toaster-oven, peel and freeze.

ASPARAGUS
Tofu
Onion

Serves 2
3 oz(100 g) frozen asparagus
⅓ cake firm *tofu*
½ onion
1½ cups *dashi* stock
1½-2 Tbsp light-colored *miso*
Shredded *shiso* leaves, optional

89 kcal per serving

1 Cut *tofu* into ¾"(2 cm) cubes, onion into the same size squares.
2 Place *dashi* stock and onion in a saucepan and bring to a boil. Add frozen asparagus and cook for 2-3 minutes until tender.
3 Add *tofu* and dissolve *miso* in stock and turn off heat as soon as it reaches the boiling point. Garnish with shredded *shiso* leaves, if preferred.

Fresh, Frozen, Dried, or Canned?

In this chapter, we introduce the advantages of using frozen foods in *miso* soups. They have already been dressed and in most cases blanched so as to save your time and effort.

Frozen or canned vegetables are often more nutrient than fresh ones purchased out of season, because they are harvested and prepared at the peak of each season. They can be even economical when fresh vegetables cost high due to unusual climate.

It would be convenient if you store a variety of emergency food in frozen, dry, or canned form. Dried ingredients include sea vegetables such as *wakame* or *nori*, and even

sliced long onion are now available in small portions. Canned tuna, corn and beans can be added to most soups and cook in no time.

Make *miso* soups with as much vegetable ingredients as you can, and stay healthy.

Note:If substituting frozen food with fresh ones, adjust the order and the time of cooking according to the size and consistency.

LOCAL SPECIALTIES

If you travel around Japan, you may encounter a soup with unforgettable flavor.
The climate of the district affects the type of *miso* soup,
creating lots of traditional combinations.
Make one at home and let your imagination run wild.

In the ancient capital of the country, there still is a tradition of making this soup on 25th of every month, the festival day for the Tenjin god of Kitano Tenman-gu Shrine. Rich *saikyo miso*, originated in Kyoto, is used. A mellow, light yellow *miso* can be used as well.

KYOTO-*MISO* SOUP
TENJIN - SAN
天神さん from **KYOTO**

Serves 2
½ fried *tofu* (*abyura-age*)
½ yam cake (*konnyaku*)
1½ cups *dashi* stock
1½-2 Tbsp *saikyo miso*

67 kcal per serving

1 Douse fried *tofu* with boiling water to remove excess oil. Then cut into wide strips. Cut yam cake likewise and parboil.
2 Place *dashi* stock and vegetable in a saucepan, and bring to a boil. Reduce heat to medium and cook for 1-2 minutes.
3 Dissolve *miso* in the stock and keep a gentle boil for another 1-2 minutes.

(**Popular Ingredients**)

Yam cake (*Konnyaku*)
Firm, jelly-like cake made from *konnyaku* potato, popular for its pleasant texture. *Konnyaku* was said to remove dirt in the body, and recently it has been proven that the dietary fiber of *konnyaku* helps activate the intestines at the same time cleaning the inside of them. Contains almost no calories.

CHICKEN AND VEGETABLE STEW

SATSUMA-JIRU

薩摩汁 from **KAGOSHIMA**

This deep-flavored dish originated in Satsuma, an old name for Kagoshima, Kyushu, and now it has become popular all over Japan. In the old days, after a cockfight, people there used to cook the defeated cock(*shamo*)soups.

Serves 2

½ lb (230 g) stewing chicken, cut up
4 oz(120 g) *daikon* radish
⅓ carrot
2 oz(60 g) *gobo* burdock
2 *satoimo* potatoes
  Salt for rubbing
½ yam cake(*konnyaku*)
1 fried *tofu*(*abura-age*)
1⅔ cups *dashi* stock
4 Tbsp barley *miso*
1 knob ginger, optional

347 kcal per serving

1 Cut *daikon* and carrot into thin rectangles.
2 Cut *gobo* into thick shavings or thin, diagonal slices. Soak in water for 15 minutes, changing water once.
3 Wash and peel *satoimo*, and cut into about ⅛"(3 mm) slices. Rub with salt to remove slipperiness. This way, *satoimo* will absorb the flavor well.
4 Cut yam cake into thin rectangles, and parboil for 5 minutes; drain. Douse fried *tofu* with boiling water, and cut into rectangles.
5 Place *dashi* stock and all ingredients in a saucepan, and bring to a boil. Reduce heat to medium, and cook for 15 minutes constantly skimming.
6 Dissolve *miso* gradually in the stock and cook over low heat for 1-2 minutes. Garnish with grated ginger, if preferred.

Why this type *miso*?

You may ask, "Do you have to buy so many kinds of *miso* for just making soup?" *Miso* has so many varieties that even most Japanese have not tasted all. Besides the common products made by major manufacturers, there are numerous labels from each district, in other words, from each climate and culture. So, the answer to the question is "No." You do not have to buy what the recipe calls for. Experiment just as you would with numerous kinds of cheese or wine.

However, it may be useful to know the characteristics of each. Roughly speaking, people in northern area prefer salty *miso* whereas milder product is favored in southern part, especially in Kansai area where people admire light and subtle flavors. It does not mean that northern people are uninterested in delicate flavor, it is just a matter of "taste." Barley *miso* is popular in the south, both sweet and salty types.

Purchase a small package of each light and dark or sweet and salty types, and blend the two depending on the ingredient. Light-colored *miso* is generally used for vegetables or in cold weather because of its richer flavor, and dark type for seafood or in summer. Just remember that *miso* is always interchangeable.

VEGETABLE STEW
GOKO-JIRU
御講汁 from **MIE**

"*Goko*" means a fun meeting of local people, and this simple vegetable stew used to be cooked in a huge pot and served to villagers who gathered at a host's house.

Serves 2
3 oz(90 g) *daikon* radish
2 oz(60 g) carrot
2 *satoimo* potatoes
2 oz(60 g) *gobo* burdock
1⅔ cups *dashi* stock
2 Tbsp dark-colored *miso*

191 kcal per serving

1 Cut all vegetables into rolling wedges (see page 89.)
2 Place *dashi* stock and all vegetables in a saucepan, and bring to a boil. Reduce heat and simmer until very tender.
3 Dissolve *miso* gradually in the stock and simmer for a further 10 minutes until vegetables absorb the *miso* flavor.

SOUP WITH EGGPLANT
DONGAME-JIRU
土亀汁 from **KYOTO**

A humorous soup with "tortoise" peeking out from a muddy pond. Small eggplant is scored crosswise to resemble a tortoise shell.

Serves 2
1 Japanese eggplant
½ fried *tofu* (*abura-age*)
1½ cups *dashi* stock
1½-2 Tbsp dark-colored *miso*

59 kcal per serving

1 Trim off top of eggplant, and split lengthwise in half. Make scores in a lattice pattern over the skin, and soak in water for 3 minutes; drain.
2 Douse fried *tofu* with boiling water to remove excess oil, and cut into julienne strips.
3 Heat *dashi* stock and eggplant to a boil, then reduce heat to medium and cook for 7-8 minutes until the eggplant is tender.
4 Dissolve *miso* gradually in the stock and cook for 1-2 minutes.

FERMENTED SOYBEAN SOUP
NATTO-JIRU
納豆汁 from **YAMAGATA**

Enjoy a country mood. Ingredients cut into tiny pieces will slip through the throat as you taste the deep flavor of *natto*, fermented soybeans.

Serves 2
3 oz(90 g) *natto* (fermented soybeans)
½ cake *tofu*
½ fried *tofu* (*abura-age*)
½ yam cake (*konnyaku*)
⅙ oz(5 g) dried stalk of *satoimo* (*imogara*), optional
1½ cups *dashi* stock
1½-2 Tbsp dark-colored *miso* with grains

207 kcal per serving

1 Crush *natto* roughly with a fork. Cut *tofu* into ⅜"× ¾"(1 cm× 2 cm) sticks.
2 Douse fried *tofu* with boiling water to remove excess oil, then cut into ⅜"(1 cm) dices. Cut yam cake into same size dices. Parboil *imogara* 1-2 minutes, then plunge into cold water. Squeeze out water and cut up.
3 Place *dashi* stock, fried *tofu*, yam cake and *imogara*, and bring to a boil. Cook 1-2 minutes. Dissolve *miso* in the stock and add *natto* and *tofu*. Return just to a boil.

THICK YAM SOUP
TORORO-JIRU
とろろ汁 from **SAITAMA**

An appetizing, velvety cold soup of grated *yamato-imo* yam, flavored with stock and *miso*.

Serves 2
3 oz(90 g) *yamato-imo* yam
  Dash vinegar
1 cup *dashi* stock
2 Tbsp dark-colored *miso*
Sliced scallions, optional

73 kcal per serving

Grated *yamato-imo* yam
(*Tororo-imo*)

1 Peel *yamato-imo*, and soak in vinegared water for 10 minutes to prevent darkening. Rinse off slipperiness under running water, and wipe dry. Grate using the sides of a mortar (*suribachi*) or a fine grater.
2 Heat *dashi* stock to a boil, gradually dissolve *miso* in it, and turn off heat. Cool until lukewarm, and add to grated yam little by little, constantly stirring to blend. Garnish with sliced scallions, if preferred.

SOUP WITH SARDINE DUMPLINGS
TSUMIRE-JIRU
つみれ汁 from **CHIBA**

Serves 2
2 medium fresh sardines
  (about 3 oz/100 g each)
  Juice of 1 knob ginger
1 Tbsp all-purpose flour
1 Tbsp Sendai *miso* or
  salty dark-colored *miso*
1⅔ cups *dashi* stock
1½-2 Tbsp dark-colored *miso*
Scallions

271 kcal per serving

Fresh sardines landed on the shores of Chiba were made into savory dumplings, or *tsumire*, enhanced with *miso* and ginger. This soup is everyone's favorite today.

1 Discard heads and insides of sardines, and wash thoroughly; pat dry. Thrust your thumb into the hollow of sardine and work along the backbone to split open. Remove backbone and skin. Slice off fine bones at the belly. Leave remaining fine bones as it will be minced and do no harm. Place in a food processor or blender with ginger juice, flour and *miso*. Blend into a paste.
2 Place *dashi* stock and bring to a boil. Using a wet spoon, scoop some sardine paste and drop into stock. Cook over medium heat for 3-4 minutes until the dumplings float to the surface.
3 Dissolve *miso* gradually in the stock and return to boil. Turn off heat and add sliced scallions.

PORK AND VEGETABLE SOUP
TON-JIRU
豚汁 from **KANTO AREA**

A hearty soup with thinly sliced pork(*ton*), and various vegetables that are in hand. This *miso* soup is also a very popular dish served outdoors in cold weathers.

Serves 2

¼ *gobo* burdock
1 oz(30 g) carrot
2 oz(60 g) sweet potato
½ long onion (Tokyo *negi*)
2 oz(60 g) thinly sliced pork
¼ cake *tofu*, diced
1⅔ cups *dashi* stock
2 Tbsp light-color *miso* with grains

152 kcal per serving

1 Scrape off skin of *gobo*, and cut into shavings. Soak in water to prevent darkening. Slice all other ingredients into thin, bite-size pieces.
2 Place *dashi* stock and bring to a boil. Add pork and heat through, removing scum. Add vegetables and cook over medium heat for 7-8 minutes.
3 Dissolve *miso* in the stock gradually, add *tofu*, and return to boil.

THICK SOUP WITH NOODLES
UCHIKOMI-JIRU
打ちこみ汁 from **KAGAWA**

This is a quite stuffing soup with *udon*, or thick noodles, which Kagawa is famous for.

Serves 2

2 *satoimo* potatoes
⅓ *gobo* burdock
1 oz(30 g) carrot
½ fried *tofu* (*abura-age*)
2 oz(60 g) *udon* noodles or
  3 oz(100 g) cooked *udon*
1⅔ cups *dashi* stock
2 Tbsp barley *miso*
Sliced scallions

247 kcal per serving

1 Peel and slice *satoimo* thinly. Cut *gobo* into halves lengthwise, then into thin, diagonal slices; soak in water. Cut carrot and *tofu* into jullienne strips.
2 Place *dashi* stock and vegetables except scallions in a saucepan, and bring to a boil. Reduce heat to medium, and cook for 7-8 minutes.
3 Add *udon* and cook for 4-5 minutes or until done if using uncooked type.
4 Dissolve *miso* in the stock and turn off heat. Garnish with scallions.

SALMON SOUP WITH *SAKE* LEE
KASU-JIRU
粕汁 from **IWATE**

Fragrant *sake* lee stimulates your appetite. Body warming treat for a cold day.

Serves 2
1 fillet salted salmon
2 oz(60 g) *daikon* radish
2 oz(60 g) carrot
2 *satoimo* potatoes
½ fried *tofu* (*abura-age*)
½ long onion (Tokyo *negi*)
3 oz(100 g) *sake* lee
2 cups *dashi* stock
2 Tbsp light-colored *miso* with grain

279 kcal per serving

1 Tear *sake* lee into small pieces, and soak in ½ cup of the stock.
2 Douse fried *tofu* with boiling water. Cut into thin rectangles. Cut *daikon* and carrot likewise. Peel and slice *satoimo* thinly; rub with salt and wash off salt to remove slipperiness. Cut salmon into bite-size pieces. Cut long onion into ¾ "(2 cm) lengths.
3 Place *dashi* stock, fried *tofu*, *daikon*, carrot, and *satoimo* in a saucepan, and bring to a boil. Add salmon, reduce heat and cook for 7-8 minutes.
4 Add long onion and *sake* lee with the liquid. Dissolve *miso* gradually in the stock and cook gently until the flavor is absorbed.

COD SOUP
DONGARA-JIRU
どんがら汁 from **YAMAGATA**

Dongara translates as bony parts of fish. This is an easy version using cod fillets.

Serves 2
2 fillets cod
2 oz(60 g) *daikon* radish
½ long onion (Tokyo *negi*)
½ cake *tofu*
1⅔ cups *dashi* stock
2 Tbsp dark-colored *miso* with grain
Seven spice mix, optional

163 kcal per serving

1 Cut cod and *tofu* into bite-size pieces, *daikon* into thin half moons. Slice long onion diagonally.
2 Place stock and *daikon* in a saucepan, and bring to a boil. Add cod pieces and heat through. Add long onion and *tofu*, and return to boil. Dissolve *miso* gradually in the stock. Sprinkle with seven spice mix, if preferred.

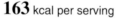

SALMON STEW
ISHIKARI NABE
石狩鍋 from HOKKAIDO

Salmon, a symbolic fish of Ishikari, Hokkaido, is cooked with vegetables on the dinner table as *nabemono*.

Serves 2
1 fillet fresh salmon
½ cake *tofu*
½ yam cake (*konnyaku*)
2 oz(60 g) *daikon* radish
2 oz(60 g) carrot
2 *shiitake* mushrooms
½ long onion (Tokyo *negi*)
1⅔ cups *dashi* stock
2 Tbsp light-colored *miso* with grains
Sansho pepper, optional

203 kcal per serving

1 Cut salmon into bite-size pieces.
2 Tear yam cake into bite-size pieces, and parboil. Cut *daikon* and carrot into thin quarter rounds. Trim off stems of *shiitake*, and slice diagonally.
3 Slice long onion diagonally, *tofu* into bite-size pieces.
4 In a saucepan place stock, yam cake, *daikon*, carrot and *shiitake*, and bring to a boil. Add salmon.
5 When salmon is heated through, add *tofu* and long onion, and cook briefly. Dissolve *miso* gradually in stock. Sprinkle with *sansho* pepper, if preferred.

Other one-pot dishes with *miso*

Nabemono, or one-pot dish, is a popular winter fare usually cooked on dinner table so as to serve directly from the steaming pot. *Sukiyaki* and *shabu-shabu* belong to this category, to name a few. Like this *Ishikari nabe*, *miso* is often added as a seasoning to enhance fish, meat, oysters, or anything with a strong flavor.

BEANS AND POTATO SOUP
ITOKO-JIRU
いとこ汁 from **KYOTO**

This simple vegetarian soup is a specialty of Kameoka, a city to the west of Kyoto.

Serves 2
- 3 oz(100 g) sweet potatoes
- 2 *satoimo* potatoes
- 2 oz(60 g) carrot
- ¼ cake *tofu*
- ¼ cup canned cooked *azuki* beans(See page 38)
- 1½ cups *dashi* stock
- 1½-2 Tbsp *akadashi miso*

157 kcal per serving

1 Cut sweet potato, *satoimo*, and carrot into ½"(1.5 cm) dices. Cut *tofu* into smaller dices.
2 In a saucepan place stock and vegetables and drained *azuki* beans, and bring to a boil. Reduce heat to medium and cook for 7-8 minutes.
3 Dissolve *miso* gradually in stock, and add *tofu*. Return to boil, and turn off heat.

BARLEY-*MISO* SOUP

DANGO-JIRU
团子汁 from **OITA**

Serves 2

2 *satoimo* potatoes
  Salt for rubbing
2 oz(60 g) carrot
3 oz(100 g) *daikon* radish
2 oz(60 g) dried *udon* noodles
1⅔ cups *dashi* stock
2 Tbsp barley *miso*

229 kcal per serving

This soup is cooked in a large pot in winter, and originally calls for *dango* (*dago* in dialect), or unique dumplings that resemble abalone. Here, they are substituted with *udon* noodles.

1 Quarter *satoimo*, and rub with salt ro remove slipperiness, and wash off salt under running water. Cut carrot and *daikon* into rolling wedges.
2 Slice long onion diagonally.
3 Cook *udon* according to the directions written on the package.
4 In a saucepan place stock and vegetables except long onion, and bring to a boil. Reduce heat to medium and cook for 7-8 minutes until tender.
5 Dissolve *miso* gradually in the stock. Add long onion, and cook for a further 2-3 minutes.

| Popular Ingredients |

Satoimo potato

Satoimo potato or yam contains little nutrients such as vitamins and dietary fiber, but its jelly-like, slippery substance is called galactan, mannan, or mucin, and turns it into an antidotal substance in the body, helping food digestion. Some areas where *satoimo* is eaten as a staple food are known for the people's longevity.

SIDE DISHES TO GIVE LIFE TO USED *DASHI* INGREDIENTS

Ingredients used to make *dashi* stock still have good flavors
and you may not want to throw them away.
Here are quick and easy side dishes that go with plain rice.

Simmered Sardines
(*Niboshi Tsukuda-ni*)

1 portion used dried
  sardines
1 Tbsp *sake*
½ Tbsp sugar
1 Tbsp soy sauce
Dash seven-spice mix

In a small saucepan, cook sardines
with the seasonings except seven-
spice mix. Stir constantly and cook
until all the liquid is absorbed.
Sprinkle with seven-spice mix.

Simmered Bonito and *Kombu*
(*Katsuo/Kombu Tsukudani*)

1 portion used dried bonito shavings
1 portion used *kombu*, sliced
1 Tbsp *sake*
1 Tbsp sugar
1½ Tbsp soy sauce

Place bonito shavings, *kombu* and the
seasonings in a small saucepan. Cook and
stir until all the liquid is absorbed.

Bonito Sprinklings
Kombu Furikake

1 portions used dried bonito flakes
2 Tbsp *sake*
1 Tbsp sugar
1½ Tbsp soy sauce
Green laver (*aonori*)
White sesame seeds

In a small saucepan place bonito flakes and the liquid seasonings.
Cook and stir over medium heat until the flakes become dry and
separate from each other. Stir in green laver and sesame seeds.

EXTRA-QUICK *MISO* SOUPS

When you spend much time for main courses,
having no time for soup, try one of these "homemade" instant soups.
Just place the ingredients in the serving bowl
and pour ½ cup or more boiling water over .

BABY SARDINES & SCALLIONS

Serves 1
½ Tbsp dried baby sardines (*jako*)
Sliced scallions
2 tsp *miso*

KOMBU SHAVINGS & SCALLIONS

Serves 1
2 Tbsp *kombu* shavings
  (*tororo kombu*)
Sliced scallions
2 tsp *miso*

DRIED SMALL SHRIMP & LONG ONION

Serves 1
1 Tbsp dried shrimp (*sakura-ebi*)
Long onion, sliced diagonally
2 tsp *miso*

TUNA & PARSLEY

Serves 1
2 Tbsp canned tuna, drained
Parsley, snipped
2 tsp *miso*

DRIED BONITO SHAVINGS & LONG ONION

Serves 1
2 Tbsp bonito shavings(*katsuobushi*)
Sliced long onion (Tokyo *negi*)
2 tsp *miso*

How about *miso* soup for lunchbox?

Dried baby sardines or shavings of dried *kombu* and bonito make a savory soup by just adding boiling water. Put a portion of such stock maker plus garnish of your choice in a sealable plastic bag, and take it with lunchbox. At lunch time, transfer the contents into your mug, and pour boiling water over them.

These "instant" *miso* soups contain less salt than the commercial ones, and do no harm to those who are on low-salt diet.

CHINESE VARIATIONS

China has various unique seasonings created by fermentation.
Their "*miso*" are called chiang and they are quite different from ours.
Here, *miso* marries popular Chinese ingredients.

TOMATO AND EGG *MISO* SOUP

The refreshing soup with fluffy eggs, enhanced with *miso*.

Serves 2
1 large tomato
1 egg, beaten
1½ cups chicken stock
1½ Tbsp dark-colored *miso*
½ tsp sesame oil

83 kcal per serving

1 Peel tomato and slice crosswise. Discard seeds, and cut into bite-size pieces.
2 Bring chicken stock to a boil, and add tomato pieces. Return to boil, then dissolve *miso* gradually. Reduce heat to low, and drizzle in beaten egg and stir lightly. Turn off heat when the egg softly sets.
3 Sprinkle with sesame oil just before serving.

(Popular Ingredients)

Nutritious value of egg
This popular ingredient is a source of perfect animal protein and a good meat substitute. Besides essential protein, it contains nearly all kinds of vitamins except vitamin C. Choose fresh ones and refrigerate with the pointed ends down so the yolks stay in the centers.

HOT AND SOUR SOUP WITH *MISO*

The famous spicy soup featuring *miso* to blend with hot bean paste, a Chinese *miso*.

Serves 2
½ cake *tofu*
½ long onion (Tokyo *negi*)
8 cloud ear fungus
1½ cups chicken stock
1 tsp hot bean paste (to-pan chiang)
1 Tbsp light-colored *miso*
1 Tbsp rice vinegar
½ tsp sesame oil

94 kcal per serving

1 Using your fingers, break *tofu* roughly, and drain.
2 Slice long onion. Soak cloud ear fungus in hot water for 5 minutes until soft and large. Trim root ends and cut up.
3 Heat chicken stock to a boil, and add *tofu* and cloud ear fungus. Also add hot bean paste.
4 Return to boil and gradually dissolve *miso* in the stock.
5 Turn off heat and sprinkle with rice vinegar and sesame oil.

Recipes using *miso*: 1   **Meat Sauce with *Miso* (*Niku-miso*)**

This is a savory, multi-purpose meat sauce popular for tacos, salads, and dips. (Serve with whole lettuce leaves, and wrap up a tablespoon of this *miso*. It is delicious!) Make a large batch and refrigerate.

INGREDIENTS: Makes 1 cup
½ lb(230 g) ground pork
1 thick, long onion (Tokyo *negi*)
1 knob ginger
5-6 fresh *shiitake* mushrooms
Seasonings to premix
  3 Tbsp *akadashi miso*
  3 tsp sugar
  2 tsp soy sauce
  1 Tbsp *sake*
  ¼ cup water
2¼ Tbsp vegetable oil
1 tsp hot bean paste (to-pan chiang)
Dash sesame oil

1 Blend seasoning to premix in a small bowl. Mince onion and ginger finely.
2 Discard stems of mushrooms, and cut into ¼"(6 mm) dices.
3 Heat vegetable oil in a wok or frying pan, and fry minced onion and ginger.
4 Add ground meat and stir constantly to crumble grains.
5 Stir in mixed seasonings and mushrooms. Bring to a boil, then reduce heat and simmer until liquid is absorbed. Adjust the seasonings to your liking.
6 When the sauce becomes glossy, stir in hot bean sauce and sesame oil; turn off heat immediately for best flavor.

Dark-colored *miso* goes with pork.

Serves 2
⅔ oz(20 g) Sichuan pickle
1 package *enoki* mushrooms
3 oz (100 g) thinly sliced lean pork
½ long onion (Tokyo *negi*)
1½ cups chicken stock
1 Tbsp dark-colored *miso*

98 kcal per serving

1 Slice Sichuan pickle very thinly, and douse with boiling water.
2 Trim off root ends of *enoki* mushrooms, and separate into clusters. Cut long onion diagonally into thin slices.
3 Place stock and sliced pickle in a saucepan, and bring to a boil. Add pork and skim. Add mushrooms and long onion.
4 Return to boil, then reduce heat. Gradually dissolve *miso* in the stock and turn off heat as soon as it reaches the boiling point.

PORK AND PICKLE *MISO* SOUP

CORN SOUP WITH *MISO*

Thick, mild-tasting soup accentuated with garlic chives.

Serves 2
5 oz (150 g) canned cream style corn
2 oz (60 g) minced chicken
  1 Tbsp *sake*
1 oz(30 g) garlic chives
1 egg, beaten
1½ cups chicken stock
1 Tbsp light-colored *miso*

200 kcal per serving

1 In a small bowl, combine minced chicken with *sake*. Slice garlic chives.
2 Heat stock to a boil, and stir in minced chicken. Stir quickly to separate grains until heated through.
3 Skim. Add creamed corn and then dissolve *miso* gradually.
4 Bring to a gentle boil, and stir in beaten egg.
5 Add garlic chives just before turning the heat off.

BEAN VERMICELLI SOUP WITH *MISO*

Smooth and delicate soup with a fragrance of ginger.

Serves 2

⅔ oz (20 g) bean vermicelli
2 oz (60 g) thinly sliced lean pork
½ long onion (Tokyo *negi*)
1 large leaf of cabbage
½ package *maitake* mushrooms
1 small knob ginger
½ Tbsp sesame oil
1½ cups chicken stock
1 Tbsp *sake*
1½ Tbsps light-colored *miso*

151 kcal per serving

1 Soak bean vermicelli in lukewarm water for 5 minutes until supple. Cut into 4"(10 cm) lengths.
2 Shred pork slices.
3 Cut long onion lengthwise in half, then into thin, diagonal slices. Shred cabbage and ginger. Separate *maitake* into clusters.
4 Heat sesame oil in a saucepan, stir-fry pork until the color turns whitish. Add vegetables and stir-fry briefly.
5 Add vermicelli, stock and *sake*, and bring to a boil. Skim and reduce heat.
6 Dissolve *miso* gradually in the stock. Turn off heat as soon as it reaches the boiling point.

SHRIMP AND CABBAGE *MISO* SOUP

Chinese dried shrimp makes a great stock, and here it is flavored with *miso* and milk, a perfect combination.

Serves 2

⅔ oz(20 g) dried shrimp
1 Tbsp *sake*
¼ cup lukewarm water
5 oz(150 g) Chinese cabbage
¾ cup chicken stock
½ cup milk
1½ Tbsp light-colored *miso*

103 kcal per serving

1 Soak dried shrimp in *sake* and lukewarm water for 30 minutes.
2 Cut Chinese cabbage, leaf into rough bite-size pieces, core into diagonal, thin slices.
3 Place stock, shrimp and soaking liquid in a saucepan, and bring to a boil. Add core of Chinese cabbage and cook until transparent. Add leaves and return to boil.
4 Add milk. Dissolve *miso* gradually in the stock, and turn off heat as soon as it reaches the boiling point.

WESTERN VARIATIONS

A spoonful of *miso* will give a deep, aromatic flavor to Western soups. Experiment in your favorite dishes by just keeping the basic principles in mind, and enjoy the possibilities of this all-purpose seasoning.

TOMATO SOUP WITH *MISO*

Refreshing chicken soup mellowed with *miso* and milk.

Serves 2
1 large tomato
½ onion
½ chicken thigh
½ Tbsp butter
1 Tbsp all-purpose flour
3 Tbsp tomato puree
1½ cups chicken stock
1 bay leaf
Nutmeg
Pepper
¼ cup milk
2 Tbsp light-colored *miso*
Green peas, optional

229 kcal per serving

1 Peel tomato by dousing with boiling water well and plunging into cold water. Halve tomato crosswise, discard seeds, and cut up.
2 Cut onion into ⅜" (1 cm) squares, chicken into ½"(1.5 cm) dices.
3 Melt butter in a saucepan, and fry diced chicken. When heated through, sprinkle with flour and stir-fry. Add tomato, tomato puree, stock, bay leaf and spices. Cook and stir over low heat for 5-6 minutes. Add green peas so add color, if preferred.
4 Add milk, then dissolve *miso* gradually by dipping a *miso* strainer in the stock (or place *miso* in a ladle, and thin it with little stock from the pan.) then dissolve evenly. Turn off heat as soon as reaching the boiling point.

POT AU FEU WITH *MISO*

Well-known French soup using lots of vegetables. *Miso* gives a deep flavor.

Serves 2
4 wieners sausages
⅙ head cabbage
½ stalk celery
½ carrot
2 small potatoes
1⅔ cups beef or chicken stock
1 Tbsp white wine
1 bay leaf
1½ Tbsp light-colored *miso*

275 kcal per serving

1 Halve cabbage into wedges, cores attached. String celery, and cut up. Cut carrot and potatoes into stewing size.
2 Place stock, wine, bay leaf, and vegetables in a saucepan, and bring to a boil. Reduce heat to low and simmer for 15-20 minutes until vegetables are fork-tender.
3 Add sausages and continue to cook for 2-3 minutes until heated through. Dissolve *miso* gradually in the stock, and turn off heat as soon as it reaches the boiling point.

Recipes using *miso*: 2

Sweet & Sour Dressing (*Sumiso*)

Great for seafood including fresh or cooked shellfish, sea vegetables, or vegetable with a strong flavor such as celery.
INGREDIENTS: Makes ½ cup
3 Tbsp light-colored *miso*
3 Tbsp rice vinegar
1 Tbsp *mirin*
1 Tbsp sugar
1 Tbsp sesame paste

1 In a bowl or blender, mix *miso*, vinegar, *mirin* and sugar until well blended.
2 Stir in vinegar and beat until smooth.

Zesty *Miso* Dressing

This rich-tasting yet light dressing enhances any vegetable and/or seafood salad including *sashimi*. If you want to make it simpler, just add sweet-type *miso* to commercial French or Italian dressing.
INGREDIENTS: Makes 1 cup
2 Tbsp *saikyo miso*
¼ cup rice vinegar
¾ cup vegetable oil
1 tsp salt
Pepper

1 In a bowl, place vinegar, salt and pepper, and stir well. Stir in *miso* gradually to mix evenly.
2 Stir in vegetable oil gradually and beat until smooth.

CLAM CHOWDER WITH *MISO*

Serves 2

3 oz(90 g) shucked hard-shell clams
1 small potato, diced
½ carrot, diced
½ onion, chopped
1 strip bacon
½ Tbsp vegetable oil
1½ cups chicken or *kombu* stock
1 bay leaf
Thyme
¼ cup milk
1½ Tbsp light-colored *miso*
Italian parsley, optional

203 kcal per serving

1 Soak diced potato in water and set aside. Slice bacon thinly.
2 Heat oil in a saucepan, fry bacon briefly, and add carrot, onion and drained potato. When vegetables are transparent, add stock, bay leaf and thyme. Bring to a boil, reduce heat to low, and cook for 7-8 minutes until vegetables are tender.
3 Add clams and milk. Dissolve *miso* gradually in the stock, and turn off heat as soon as it reaches the boiling point. Garnish with sprigs of Italian parsley, if preferred.

Miso makes this famous soup even milder.

FRENCH ONION SOUP WITH *MISO*

Browned onion and *miso* make a deep aroma.

Serves 2

1 large onion
1 Tbsp butter
1½ cups beef stock
1 bay leaf
Dash grated garlic
Pepper
1 Tbsp *akadashi miso*
2 thin slices French bread
1¾ oz(50 g) Swiss cheese
Parsley, minced

287 kcal per serving

1 Slice onion into fine slices.
2 Melt butter in a saucepan, and fry onion over medium heat until dry. Reduce heat to low, and stir-fry for 15-20 minutes until onion is golden. Do not burn them.
3 Add stock, bay leaf, grated garlic and pepper, and bring to a boil over high heat. Dissolve *miso* gradually in the stock.
4 Grease individual bowls and place bread slices. Spoon in the soup and top with grated cheese. Grill in preheated oven until brown, and sprinkle with parsley.

Serves 2

½ onion, diced
½ stalk celery, diced
1 Japanese, or ¼ regular eggplant, diced
4 button mushrooms, quartered
1 large tomato
½ Tbsp olive oil
1¾ cups chicken or veal stock
2 Tbsp white wine
Thyme
Dash grated garlic
1 oz(30 g) short pasta
1½ Tbsp dark-colored *miso*

164 kcal per serving

1 Soak diced eggplant in water. Peel tomato (p 84,#1), halve crosswise, discard seeds, then cut up.
2 Fry diced vegetables in heated olive oil. Add tomato, stock, wine and spices. Bring to a boil, skim, and add pasta.
3 When pasta is cooked, dissolve *miso* gradually in the stock, and turn off heat as soon as it reaches the boiling point.

MINESTRONE WITH *MISO*

Short pasta can be added directly to the pot.

PUMPKIN SOUP WITH *MISO*

Carotene-rich, country-style soup using roughly mashed, unpeeled pumpkin.

Serves 2
5 oz(150 g) pumpkin
½ onion, chopped
½ Tbsp butter
1 cup chicken stock
1 bay leaf
Pepper
1 cup milk
1½ Tbsp dark-colored *miso*

186 kcal per serving

1 Discard seeds from pumpkin and cut into bite-size pieces.
2 Melt butter in a saucepan, and fry onion until supple. Add pumpkin and stir-fry briefly. Add stock, bay leaf and pepper, bring to a boil, then reduce heat to low. Simmer until pumpkin is tender.
3 Remove from heat. Discard bay leaf, and crush pumpkin roughly.
4 Return to heat and add milk and *miso*. When beginning to boil, turn off heat immediately.

Cutting Techniques

An ingredient may taste different depending on its shape and size especially when cooked. Also, in order to make *miso* soup quickly in one pot, it is important to cut the vegetables into small and most appropriate shapes so they can be ready almost in the same period of time. Peel, if necessary, before cutting.

〖HALF MOONS〗

Round slices cut into halves

Cut lengthwise in half.

Cut crosswise into appropriate widths.

〖QUARTER MOONS〗

Quartered slices

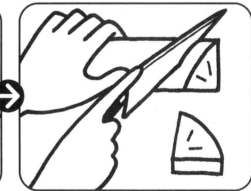

Cut lengthwise into quarters.

Cut crosswise into appropriate widths.

〖RECTANGLES〗

Thick rectangles suitable for *daikon,* carrot, etc.

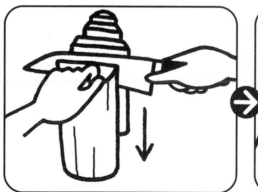

Place cylindrical cut of required length, cut-edge facing down, and slice into thick pieces.

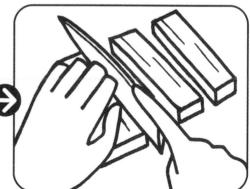

Cut each piece lengthwise (along grains) into appropriate widths.

【STRIPS/SHREDS】

Suitable for *daikon*, carrot, ginger. The term depends on thickness: thicker sticks are called strips

Place cylindrical cut, flat edge facing down, and slice thinly along the grains.

Cut along the grains into required thicknesses.

【ROLLING WEDGES】

This cutting gives ingredients maximum surfaces to absorb flavors. Suitable for carrot, eggplant, potatoes, yams, *daikon*, etc.

Cut diagonally across the cut edge, then roll to cut in the same manner.

If the vegetable is too thick, split lengthwise in half, then cut as for the left.

【WEDGES】

Here is a special wedge cutting for onion, to reduce cooking time

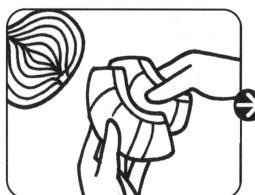

Cut into halves along the grains, cut off the bottom, then separate the layers.

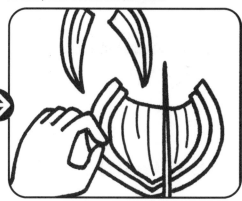

Layer 2-3 pieces and cut into same center widths.

【SHAVINGS】

· Here is a special sliver cutting for *gobo* burdock, enlarging the surface so as to hold the flavor well

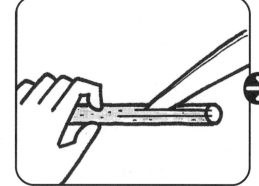

Scrape off skin with the back of knife. Make deep incision into thick part.

Using the top part of knife, shave off burdock, rolling it as you go, and dropping into water to prevent darkening.

FREEZING INGREDIENTS FOR *MISO* SOUP

【VEGETABLES】

The knack of saving vegetable is to blanch and divide into portions before putting them in the freezer. Carrot, pumpkin, and greens like spinach or *komatsuna* can be added directly to boiling stock, without thawing. It is a good idea to shred and freeze garnishes such as scallion or *yuzu* citron which adds to the soup fragrance and color.

To prepare spinach

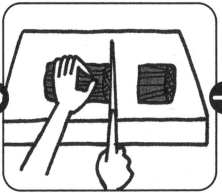

In boiling water, cook spinach just until cooked. Avoid overcooking.

Plunge into cold water, squeeze out, and cut into bite-size lengths.

Divide into portions and wrap each in a plastic film. Store in the freezer.

【SEAFOOD】

Fresh fish should be cut into pieces and wrapped one by one in a plastic film. Fresh shellfish should be divided into portions to be wrapped. Uncooked seafood becomes soggy when thawed, so be sure to dry with paper toweling before adding to stock. Squid, prawns and shrimp do not need thawing if prepared and cooked before being wrapped.

To prepare prawns or shrimp

Shell and devein prawns.

In a small amount of boiling water, cover and cook prawns.

Wrap portion by portion in a plastic film. Store in the freezer.

【MEATS AND POULTRY】

In order to use frozen meat, it is recommended that you slice to slice very thinly and wrap one piece at a time. This way the meat will soon be softened enough to be cut and add to the soup. Chicken should be cooked before being frozen. Ground meats will not deteriorate much if cooked and then cooled.

To prepare chicken

In a pot, place chicken and small amount of *sake* or dry sherry, and let steam until done.

Shred or tear chicken into strips.

Wrap one portion at a time in a plastic film, and store in the freezer.

To prepare ground meat

In an unheated pot, place small amount of sake or dry sherry with ground meat, and separate grains.

Turn on heat and cook, constantly stirring to crumble meat.

When cooled, wrap portion by portion in a plastic film, and store in the freezer.

【OTHERS】

Bacon and ham will be easy to use if wrapped one slice each or separated. Canned beans can be frozen until use. Among all processed food, *abura-age*, or fried *tofu*, is best for freezing.

To prepare fried *tofu*

 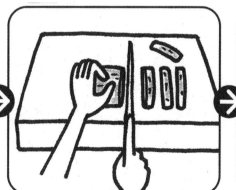 

Douse fried *tofu* with boiling water.

Cut into strips or required size.

Wrap in a plastic film, one portion at a time. Store in the freezer.

GLOSSARY

Abura-age——Thin deep-fried *tofu*. This fluffy type fried *tofu* is mainly used for simmered dishes since the deep-fried outside absorbs flavors than regular *tofu*. It is often added to *miso* soups, and also is made into pouches for *inari-zushi*, a vegetarian *sushi*.

Ashitaba **greens**——See page 23.

Atsu-age——Thick deep-fried *tofu* with less moisture than regular *tofu*. It is grilled or simmered just like the thin type.

Azuki **beans**——See page 38.

Bamboo shoot——*Takenoko*. One of the most common ingredients in Asian cooking. Fresh bamboo shoot is a spring delicacy while boiled and canned ones are available all through the year.

Cloud ear fungus——Crunchy black mushroom usually sold in dried form. It is soaked in hot water until softened, before being cooked with other ingredients.

Daikon **radish**——Large white radish, 10"-20"(25 cm-50 cm) long, 3"-4"(7.5cm-10cm) thick. This radish is a must for Japanese tables and is eaten in numerous ways such as pickling, frying, and simmering, besides being grated to make condiments.

Dashi——A basic stock widely used in Japanese cooking. *Kombu*(giant kelp) and dried bonito flakes are cooked briefly in boiling water, and then removed to make a clear broth. Today busy cooks prefer using powdered or granulated form, now available in sachets. (See page 12 - 13 for more details)

Eggplant——Japanese-type eggplant are smaller in size and have tenderer texture and skin. Be careful about the amount if using Western type.

Enoki **mushroom**——Clusters of thin white mushrooms with tiny caps and long, narrow stems, cultivated in the similar condition as the common button mushrooms. They have a delicate flavor and pleasant crispness.

Fu——Tiny round cakes with a fine, spongy texture. Popular ingredient for light soups and simmered dishes. Made from wheat protein, *fu* is easily digested and nutritious. Soak in water and squeeze before cooking.

Ganmodoki——Deep-fried *tofu* dumpling used in simmered dishes. Soft, fried surface holds flavors well.

Ginger root——Ginger is used only in fresh form in Asian cooking. Look for firm rhizomes.

Gobo **burdock**——Fibrous burdock roots prized for distinctive fragrance and crunchy texture. To avoid darkening and harsh taste, *gobo* should be submerged in water immediately after cutting. Change water 2-3 times until the water is clear.

Goya——See page 21.

Iriko——*Niboshi*, or dried young sardines for making *dashi* stock.

Ito-konnyaku——Yam cake cut into long strips.

Jaozi——See page 61

Kabu——Japanese type turnip which has a tenderer and smoother texture compared to western type. It cooks fast and creates a delicate flavor when cooked or pickled.

Katsuobushi **or** *Kezuribushi*——Dried bonito shavings now sold in small pouches. This is the main ingredient for making *dashi* stock, but is also used as a garnish or topping to add flavor to various Japanese dishes.

Kimchee——Korean word meaning "pickles." Spicy and sour, pickled Chinese cabbage eaten daily in Korea.

Kinome——Sprig of *sansho*, or Japanese pepper, which releases a strong fragrance and makes a decorative garnish for springtime dishes.

Kiriboshi daikon——See page 21.

Koji——A natural sweetner known as an important element making for *miso*. Rice, barley, soy sauce, or bran is steamed and then fermented by *koji*(Aspergillus), which changes the starch such grains into a glucide. *Koji* yeast comes in a pressed cake form, refrigerated in shops. Choose a young cake in a snowy white color.

Kombu kelp——Dried giant kelp mainly used to make *dashi* stock. It is cut into desired size with scissors and added to cold water.

Konnyaku——See page 68.

Koya-dofu——See page 30.

Long onion——Tokyo *negi* or *naganegi*. Thick, long onion used widely in Asian cooking. It looks similar to leek, but its flavor resembles spring onion or green onion.

Maitake **mushroom**——See page 42.

Mirin——A thick, sweet wine made from rice, used primarily in cooking. It gives rich flavor and glaze to food such as *teriyaki*. If not in hand, substitute with *sake* and sugar, in a ratio of 2:1.

Mitsuba——Trefoil, a member of the parsley family. This herb has a delicate fragrance, somewhere between sorrel and celery, and is used to accent many Japanese dishes.

Myoga——Young, pinkish fresh ginger flower head, treasured as a special summer herb. It has a distinctive fragrance which enhances various salads, soups and pickles. Also good for *tempura*.

Nameko **mushroom**——Tiny, yellow to reddish brown mushroom with glutenous cap. The jelly-like substance that covers the brown cap is said to protect the walls of your stomach from strong acid or salt irritation. *Nameko* mushroom, however, has been loved for its smooth texture and delicate flavor, rather than for its health effect. Available in cans or plastic bags.

Natto——Fermented soybeans with a sticky texture and strong aroma. Some Westerners may take some time to acquire the taste. It is a great source of protein and vitamin K, and usually served with sliced scallion, hot mustard and soy sause.

Nira——Garlic chives. Flat, fleshy and soft greens with a strong garlic flavor, used for egg dishes, dim sums and soups.

Nori **seaweed**——Known as a wrapper for *sushi*, this edible blackish sea vegetable comes in dried, thin sheets. Needs to be stored in an airtight container.

Rice vinegar——Mild vinegar made from rice. Besides using for flavoring *sushi* and dressings, it is added to water in order to retain the colors of ingredients. For such preparatory use, it can be substituted with any white vinegar.

Sake——Rice wine. Known as a popular Japanese beverage, *sake* also plays a major role in Japanese cooking. It is used to remove unpleasant odors of meat or fish, and to soften meat or vegetables quickly, as well as to give a delicate flavor to most dishes. Once opened, *sake* should be kept in a cool, dark place just like wines.

Sake **lees**——*Nerikasu*, or *sake* lees paste. The dregs from making *sake* is pressed, then softended. *Sake* lees has been popular for its subtle fragrance of *sake* and natural sweetness.

Sansho **pepper**——Japanese pepper. Powdered form of *sansho* fruit, used as a spice.

Satoimo **potato**——Japanese taro with a much finer, smoother texture. A popular ingredient for *miso* soup and simmered dishes.

Sesame oil——An essential, fragrant oil favored in most Asian cooking. Sesame oil has a nutty flavor and is mainly used for flavoring food rather than frying.

Seven spice mix——An aromatic ready-mix of seven Japanese spices: red pepper, *sansho* pepper, green *nori* seaweed, white sesame seeds, citrus peel, linen seeds and poppy seeds.

Shiitake **mushroom**——Chinese black mushrooms available in fresh or dried form. It is reported that *shiitake* helps lowering high blood pressure or risk of cancer.

Shimeji **mushroom**——Clusters of grey-capped, white mushrooms prized for their flavor.

Shiso——Perilla leaves in green or purple-red color. This herb is related to the mint family and has a pleasant aroma. Green *shiso* is mainly used for cooking or as a condiment for *sashimi* platters while red *shiso* is often added to pickled vegetables.

Soy sauce——A salty, dark-brown colored sauce made by fermenting soybeans in brine. Choose clear-colored product. Once opened, soy sauce doesn't keep many months, and should be kept in a cool, dark place.

Tofu——Soybean curd. *Tofu* is rich in proteins, vitamins and minerals, and is entirely free of cholesterol because of the low content of saturated fat. *Tofu* cakes should be kept in water, which should be changed daily.

To-pan chiang——Chinese seasoning known as hot bean paste. It is made from soy beans, chili peppers and sometimes garlic. Comes in jars or cans.

Tororo——See page 71.

Tsumire——See page 72.

Udon **noodles**——Wheat noodles which come in various thicknesses. Available in dried or fresh form.

Yamato-imo——Mountain yam favored for its glutenous, smooth texture and nutritious value. To prevent darkening, *yamato-imo* is soaked for about 10 minutes in vinegared water after it is peeled.

Notes:

1 cup = 240 ml

1 teaspoon(tsp) = 5 ml

1 tablespoon(Tbsp) = 15 ml

INDEX

ACKNOWLEDGMENTS

Supervisor: Satomi Kenmizaki

Translator: Yoko Ishiguro

Cooking Staff: Nozomi Niikura

Photographer: Yasunori Komatsu

Illustrator: Kyoko Nonomura

Project Editor: Juwaki

English Editor: Mieko Baba